MATT AND TOM OLDFIELD

## ULTIMATE
## FOOTBALL HEROES

# COUTINHO

## FROM THE PLAYGROUND
## TO THE PITCH

**DINO**

Published by Dino Books,
an imprint of John Blake Publishing,
2.25, The Plaza,
535 Kings Road,
Chelsea Harbour,
London SW10 0SZ

www.johnblakepublishing.co.uk

www.facebook.com/johnblakebooks 🟦
twitter.com/jblakebooks 🟦

This edition published in 2017

ISBN: 978 1 78606 462 2

British Library Cataloguing-in-Publication Data:

A catalogue record for this book is available from the British Library.

Design by www.envydesign.co.uk

Printed and bound in Great Britain by Clays Ltd, Elcograf S.p.A.

5 7 9 10 8 6

Papers used by John Blake Publishing are natural, recyclable products made from
wood grown in sustainable forests. The manufacturing processes conform to the
environmental regulations of the country of origin.

Every attempt has been made to contact the relevant copyright-holders, but some
were unobtainable. We would be grateful if the appropriate people could contact us.

John Blake Publishing is an imprint of Bonnier Publishing
www.bonnierpublishing.com

*For Noah and Nico,*
*Southampton's future strikeforce*

ULTIMATE
FOOTBALL HEROES

Matt Oldfield is an accomplished writer and the editor-in-chief of football review site Of Pitch & Page. Tom Oldfield is a freelance sports writer and the author of biographies on Cristiano Ronaldo, Arsène Wenger and Rafael Nadal.

Cover illustration by Dan Leydon.
To learn more about Dan visit danleydon.com
To purchase his artwork visit etsy.com/shop/footynews
Or just follow him on Twitter @danleydon

# TABLE OF CONTENTS

# ACKNOWLEDGEMENTS

First of all, I'd like to thank John Blake Publishing – and particularly my editor James Hodgkinson – for giving me the opportunity to work on these books and for supporting me throughout. Writing stories for the next generation of football fans is both an honour and a pleasure.

I wouldn't be doing this if it wasn't for Tom. I owe him so much and I'm very grateful for his belief in me as an author. I feel like Robin setting out on a solo career after a great partnership with Batman. I hope I do him (Tom, not Batman) justice with these new books.

Next up, I want to thank my friends for keeping

me sane during long hours in front of the laptop.
Pang, Will, Mills, Doug, John, Charlie – the laughs
and the cups of coffee are always appreciated.

I've already thanked my brother but I'm also very
grateful to the rest of my family, especially Melissa,
Noah and of course Mum and Dad. To my parents, I
owe my biggest passions: football and books. They're
a real inspiration for everything I do.

Finally, I couldn't have done this without Iona's
encouragement and understanding during long,
work-filled weekends. Much love to you.

**CHAPTER 1**

# LIVERPOOL'S MAGICIAN

Philippe took a deep breath, shut his eyes and listened to the Anfield roar. The Liverpool stadium had the best atmosphere in the whole wide world.

*Walk on, walk on*
*With hope in your heart,*
*And you'll never walk alone.*
*You'll never walk alone!*

That song gave him goosebumps every time – and so did that banner. As Philippe opened his eyes again, he looked around the stadium for it. There it was, right in the middle of the famous Kop. It showed a picture of Philippe pointing up at the sky, with '10 COUTINHO' on the back of his Liverpool shirt. And below, there were two Portuguese words. 'O Mágico': 'The Magician'. It was the best gift that he had ever been given.

Liverpool needed their magician today. It was Philippe's favourite game of the season: the Merseyside derby. He had a brilliant goalscoring record against Everton and he was determined to keep that going. Liverpool were chasing a Top 4 finish that would get them back into the Champions League again. That was Philippe's number one aim.

'Come on, let's do this!' he said to himself, stretching out his legs. Philippe and his teammate Roberto Firmino had just been all the way to Brazil to play for their national team but they were back and ready for the big match.

Philippe had started the season brilliantly but after an injury, he had struggled to regain his superstar form. It was time to put that behind him and focus on leading Liverpool to victory. This was supposed to be his season, the year when he became a consistently world-class playmaker. There was still time to achieve that.

As soon as the game kicked off, Philippe was bright and busy. He was playing on the left side of the Liverpool attack but he didn't stay there. He was everywhere. As Sadio Mané dribbled forward, Philippe sprinted across towards the middle of the penalty area. The Everton defenders followed him and that gave Sadio the space to run to the left and score. 1-0!

'Thanks, great movement!' Sadio said, giving his teammate a high-five.

Philippe was just getting started. With a burst of speed, he weaved past one defender and then another. The Liverpool fans were up on their feet, cheering his name. They loved to watch his crazy, mazy dribbles. As he entered the box, an Everton player finally managed to tackle him.

'Next time!' Philippe thought to himself as he chased back to defend.

Everton's young right-back Matthew Pennington just couldn't deal with Philippe's skill. The Brazilian glided past him again, as if he wasn't even there, but his shot was saved by the keeper. The goal was coming; Philippe felt dangerous every time he got the ball.

Idrissa Gueye tried to tackle him but his feet were far too quick. As he burst into the penalty area, Philippe faked to go left and Phil Jagielka fell for the trick. With a classic drop of the shoulder, Philippe cut right and found the space that he needed. He curled his shot beautifully into the top-right corner.

*Goooooooooooooooooooooooooooaaaaaaaaaaaaallll llllllllllllllllllllll!!!!!!!!!!!!!!!*

He was back! As he ran to the corner flag, Philippe pumped his fists and screamed. It felt so good to be scoring great goals for Liverpool again.

'Magical!' his manager, Jürgen Klopp, cheered at the break, giving him a big hug. 'We need more of that in the second half!'

Philippe had four Everton players around him but they weren't getting the ball off him today. He dribbled down the left wing, looking for the perfect pass to play. When the moment arrived, he slipped the ball into Divock Origi's path. The striker didn't even need to take a touch before shooting. 3-1!

'What a ball!' Divock shouted as they celebrated. Surely that was enough to win the derby.

As Philippe came off the pitch, the Liverpool fans gave him a standing ovation and sang his song:

*Olé Olé Olé Olé*
*Coutinho-o-o! Coutinho-o-o!*

Their Little Magician had given his all and delivered another match-winning performance against their local rivals. Klopp was clapping too.

'Phew, it's great to have you back to your best!' the Liverpool manager said happily after the match. 'Just in time for our end-of-season push.'

A week later, against Stoke City, Liverpool were losing 1-0. At half-time, the Brazilian Boys came on. Could Philippe and Roberto rescue their team? Of course they could! Twenty minutes later, the ball fell to Philippe just inside the penalty area. There were defenders running towards him but he didn't panic and smash it over the bar. That wasn't Philippe's style. Instead, he stayed calm and fired his shot right into the bottom corner. It was so precise that the goalkeeper had no chance.

*Goooooooooooooooooooooooooaaaaaaaaaaaaaaaaa aallllllllllllllllllllllllllllllll!!!!!!*

Liverpool were back in the game. Philippe raised his hands to the fans, urging them to make more noise. 'We can win this!' he shouted.

In the moment, Philippe forgot about his big achievement; with that goal he had become the highest scoring Brazilian in Premier League history. But after the match, once Roberto had scored the winner, he celebrated with his teammates and his wife, Aine.

'And I'm still only twenty-four!' Philippe laughed. Sometimes he felt much older than that.

With the support of Aine and his family, he had left Brazil at the age of just eighteen to pursue his European football dream. After spells in Italy and Spain, he had made England his home – or Liverpool, to be specific. Most Brazilians didn't stay long in England but Philippe wasn't most Brazilians.

He was a Premier League superstar and he had even beaten his good friend Neymar to win the Best Brazilian Player in Europe award for 2016.

Philippe had just signed a big new five-year contract at Anfield. He was determined to bring glory back to Merseyside. After his frustrating time at Inter Milan, Liverpool Football Club had shown faith in him and given him his confidence back. The fans loved Philippe and he loved them back. The Little Magician wasn't going anywhere.

## CHAPTER 2

# ROCHA

The Coutinhos lived in Rocha in the north of Rio de
Janeiro, Brazil. José Carlos and Esmerelda's home
was a simple place near some of the poorest areas of
the city. They didn't have a lot of money but they
did have a happy family. Their two elder sons,
Cristiano and Leandro, could be noisy, moody
teenagers at times, but they always looked after their
baby brother, Philippe.

'Go on, kick it!' Cristiano said, placing a tiny soft
football in front of Philippe's tiny right foot.

As Leandro was holding Philippe's arms because he
couldn't walk yet, Cristiano made a kicking action,
hoping that his baby brother would copy it. 'Kick!'

Philippe wiggled his foot forward. The ball didn't move very far but his brothers were pleased with his progress.

'Dad, he's going to be a star!' Leandro cheered.

José Carlos smiled. He loved football; he was *Brazilian*, after all. He had always wanted to pass on his passion to his sons but he never pushed them. He worked hard as an architect to give his children the best opportunities in life, and he encouraged them to choose their own interests.

'Be brave and try new things,' he liked to tell them.

But when it came to football, none of them needed pushing. Cristiano, Leandro and Philippe all started playing when they were very young and they never stopped. They didn't choose football; football chose them. It was a way of life in Brazil, especially if you lived near Rio de Janeiro's massive Maracanã stadium, completed in time for the 1950 World Cup, where Brazil would lose the final to Uruguay.

If one of Rio's big teams – Flamengo or Vasco da Gama – was playing there, the Coutinhos could hear the crowd roar from outside their home. They could usually tell what the score was just by listening.

'Do you like all that noise, little guy?' José Carlos asked Philippe, pulling funny faces. 'Do you think someone has scored a goal?'

His youngest son couldn't answer but he giggled and dribbled instead.

'Yes, he's definitely another football fan!' José Carlos told Esmerelda proudly.

As soon as Philippe could walk and run, he had a football glued to his foot. His brothers helped him to practise his kicking in the house, but that was as far as he was allowed to go.

'Sorry Phil, you have to stay here,' Cristiano and Leandro said, as they headed over to the concrete pitch nearby to play with their friends and have lots of fun.

When his brothers left him behind, Philippe always burst out crying. He wanted to follow them everywhere. Why couldn't he do everything that they did?

'You're too young!' Esmerelda told her son, holding him until he calmed down. 'As soon as you turn five, I promise that you can go with them. Then you can play football all day long!'

In the meantime, Philippe ran and ran. The house became his obstacle course: a chair here, a bin there, a door handle there. He bumped his head a lot but he always got back up and carried on. Once he could race around really quickly, changing direction in a flash, he added a new element – his little football. At first, dribbling slowed him down but soon he was a natural.

'Careful!' Esmerelda shouted as he whizzed past. She couldn't wait for him to turn five.

When his fifth birthday finally arrived, Philippe was allowed to go with his brothers to the concrete pitch, but that still didn't mean that he was allowed to join in the game.

'Sorry, bro, you're not ready to play with the big boys yet,' Leandro put it bluntly.

'How about being the ball boy instead?' Cristiano suggested, as if that was a really kind offer.

Philippe thought about storming off home to tell his mum but no – that would only make him look like more of a baby. Instead, he stood on the sidelines and watched. The game did look scary. The boys were all much older and stronger and they often pushed and kicked each other as they tried to win the ball.

'Am I ready for this?' Philippe asked himself. He really wanted to play but maybe it was best to just watch for now.

There was still so much for him to learn about passing, tackling and teamwork. He was determined to get everything right. When he finally got his chance to play, Philippe wanted to impress his brothers, not let them down.

'I'm going to be the best player in town!' he told himself.

Sometimes his dad came down to watch and Philippe got the chance to practise the new skills that he had learnt.

'As you kick the ball, look up at me,' José Carlos said to his son. 'That way, the ball will go exactly where you want it to go. That's the idea anyway!'

Philippe's first few passes went too wide but he

soon improved. His dad clapped and cheered.

'Great work! You'll soon be ready to play with your brothers.'

Philippe beamed; that was his dream. 'You really think so? I want to be just like them when I'm older!'

They stopped to watch as Cristiano missed a golden chance to score. 'Really?' José Carlos laughed. 'I think you could be much better than those two!'

## CHAPTER 3

# BIG BOY BROTHERS

Once Philippe turned six years old, he was ready. He was bored of standing on the side of the concrete pitch, watching the older boys play. It was his turn now. Every morning, he practised on the pitch before the others arrived. Usually, he moved when the big boys' game began but one day, he didn't.

'What are you doing?' Leandro shouted. His younger brother was embarrassing him in front of his friends.

'I want to play,' Philippe replied firmly.

Leandro rolled his eyes. 'Cristiano, tell him – he can't play because he's too small!'

Cristiano looked at his youngest brother. There was a very serious look on his face and his little fists were clenched tightly. Philippe wasn't going to move unless they dragged him away, kicking and screaming.

'How many players have we got at the moment?' Cristiano asked.

Leandro did a quick head count. 'Seven, but you can't be serious, he—'

Cristiano was the oldest boy there, so he made the rules. 'Phil, you're on my team, with Dani and Junior. Let's play!'

As the sides argued about positions and tactics, Cristiano gave Philippe a special team-talk.

'I know that you're ready for this but you've got to show the others, especially Leandro. Remember, it's not your skills that he's worried about. He knows that you can play football but he thinks that you're going to get hurt or have a tantrum.'

'I won't, I promise,' Philippe said immediately.

'Good, well let's make sure that we're the happy ones at the dinner table tonight!'

Philippe's heart was racing. He was no longer afraid of the flying tackles but he *was* afraid of letting his brothers down. Now that he was playing with the

big boys, he had to prove that he was a big boy too.
That wouldn't be easy.

At first, he chased around the pitch like a headless
chicken. Eventually, the ball came to him.

'Pass! Pass!' Dani shouted at him.

Philippe was so tired and panicky that the ball
got stuck under his foot. Dani groaned but Cristiano
ran over and had a quick word with his brother.
'Don't worry about him – slow down and just take
your time.'

Philippe was used to beating imaginary defenders
and shooting past imaginary goalkeepers. It turned
out that football was a lot harder when there were
real opponents. Especially when the real opponents
were nearly double your size.

'No foul!' Leandro shouted as he dribbled away
with the ball and left his younger brother lying
on the concrete with a bleeding knee. Cristiano
shrugged and Philippe picked himself up and carried
on. There was no point complaining.

The next time Philippe got the ball, he took a
touch and played a simple pass to Dani. That calmed

him down and gave him confidence. Soon he was working nice passing triangles with Dani and Junior. They were moving up the pitch towards the opposition goal.

'Nice football!' Cristiano shouted from defence.

Philippe had the ball on the left; he couldn't mess this up now. But there wasn't much space to move and there were big defenders everywhere. Philippe pretended that he was on his own again, playing against imaginary people. What would he usually do next? He dropped his shoulder and cut inside. Then he faked to pass right and, as Rodrigo moved to intercept, Philippe poked the ball into the bottom-left corner.

*Goooooooooooooooooooooaaaaaaaaaaaaaaaaaaaaall llllllllllllllllllllllllllllllll!!!!!!!!!*

Dani and Junior ran to congratulate him but Philippe played it cool. It was only his first proper goal ever – no big deal! He would celebrate properly later, when everyone else had gone home. When he was alone, he could go crazy.

In the end, his team lost the match but Philippe

was still buzzing. He was a footballer now and he couldn't wait to play again. When the other players left to go home, Philippe stayed behind.

'I'm just going to practise a couple of shots,' he lied.

'Okay, but don't be long,' Cristiano warned. 'Mum will be mad if the dinner gets cold!'

Once they had gone, Philippe lifted his shirt over his head and ran the full length of the pitch with his arms stretched wide like aeroplane wings.

'Yeeeeeeeeeeeeeeeeeeeeeeeeeessssssssssssssssssssssssssss sssssssssssssss!' he roared at the top of his voice.

Once that was done, Philippe went straight home.

'Was that you?' Leandro asked as he came through the front door.

'What?'

'That loud cheering sound we just heard – was that you?'

Philippe put on his best confused face. 'What loud cheering sound? I didn't hear anything.'

There was always a noisy discussion at the Coutinho dinner table. That night, it was all about their football match.

'You guys played well as a team but we had better individual players,' Leandro argued.

'I'm not sure about that,' Cristiano argued back. The brothers hardly ever agreed about anything. 'We missed a lot of chances – we should have won that game!'

José Carlos always encouraged the debates. He liked to get his sons thinking. 'Do you think the score would have changed if you'd played for longer?' he asked.

Philippe waited impatiently for the conversation to end. He had something important to say. 'Dad, I played today and I scored.'

José Carlos smiled and raised his wine glass. 'To our new football hero. Was it a good goal?'

Philippe couldn't answer the question because his brothers got there first.

'Rodrigo should really have saved it,' Leandro argued. 'I don't know why he moved across–'

'He moved across because Philippe fooled him!' Cristiano argued back. 'It was a clever goal. Well done, bro!'

Philippe was delighted to hear those three little words.

## CHAPTER 4

# *FUTSAL* FUN

Once Philippe started, there was no stopping him. In no time at all, he became the king of the concrete pitch. Cristiano and Leandro hated to admit it but their youngest brother was already a better footballer than them and he was only eight. But they didn't feel too bad because he was better than pretty much every kid in Rocha.

'The three of us against all of you!' was the challenge and, 99 per cent of the time, the Coutinho brothers still won.

At school, Philippe was introduced to a slightly different ball game – *futsal*. It was as if the game was invented just for him. With his quick feet and great touch, he could control the smaller, heavier ball perfectly. And the *futsal* court was about the same size as the concrete pitch near Philippe's house. He already knew how to escape from defenders in tight spaces.

'The only real difference,' he told his dad happily, 'is that I can play *futsal* even if it's really hot or really cold outside, because it's an indoor pitch.'

Philippe's team won game after game thanks to him. Other kids often slipped on the hard court and found it hard to turn, but Philippe had perfect balance. Even at full speed, he could dummy the keeper or dodge a tackle.

José Carlos and Esmerelda usually sat in the stands to watch Philippe play. They were pleased to see their son enjoying himself. As long as he was doing well in class, he could have all the fun he wanted.

'Did you see that shot? He's good!' José Carlos would sometimes say to his wife but, other than that, they didn't really think about Philippe's *futsal*, or football, future. Not yet.

But their son kept getting better and better. With

the ball apparently stuck to his foot, Philippe would often dribble past an entire team before scoring. It was like he had superpowers. For a boy so small, he had so much power in his kick.

After one match, José Carlos started chatting to the grandmother of one of Philippe's teammates.

'Nico's dad is trying to get him into a football academy,' the woman said. 'There are so many trials and so many disappointments. Is Philippe already at an academy?'

José Carlos shook his head. 'No, we haven't really talked to him about that yet. He loves playing *futsal* and he's really happy here. There's no rush for him to go anywhere else.'

The grandmother was shocked. 'You mean the scouts haven't discovered him yet?'

José Carlos shook his head again.

'Wow, and I thought Brazilians were meant to be the best in the world at finding young football talent!' she laughed, but then she became serious. 'Philippe is a fantastic player. I reckon the big clubs would be desperate to sign him.'

The clubs in Rio de Janeiro didn't get much bigger than Vasco da Gama. Two of Brazil's top strikers, Edmundo and Romário, had both played there. When José Carlos started asking about football academies for Philippe, Vasco da Gama sent someone to watch him play.

The Vasco youth coach turned up at a big schools tournament but Philippe didn't know it at the time. That was probably a good thing. He was just one of more than a hundred kids there, all hoping to impress the big club scouts. He had to do something very special to stand out from the crowd.

As the youth coach waited for Philippe to play, he watched the other games going on. There were lots of decent youngsters but Vasco didn't want *decent* youngsters. They wanted *exceptional* youngsters. The youth coach was looking for someone magical to catch his eye.

'Let's see if his dad's right about him,' he muttered to himself. He was used to parents exaggerating their kid's talent.

Finally, Philippe and his teammates ran out

onto the court. They high-fived each other and took up their positions. It didn't take a genius to work out who the star player was. From the moment that the game kicked off, Philippe ran the show. When he passed the ball, he moved into space to get it back again. He was never off the ball for long.

A teammate played a long ball and Philippe chased after it. As he caught up with it, the goalkeeper came out to the edge of his area to put him off. It didn't work. Philippe faked to shoot but let the ball slide across him. With the keeper lying on the ground, he ran on for an easy tap-in.

*Goooooooooooooooooooooooooooaaaaaaaaaaaaaa aaaaaaaaallllllllllllll!!!!!!!!!!!!*

The youth coach made a note – 'clever player, nice balance'.

Philippe dribbled, he passed, he flicked, he played one-twos. The only things that he didn't do were lose the ball and make a mistake. His masterclass continued right up until the referee blew the final whistle. By then, the youth coach had stopped taking notes. The last one read: 'Head and shoulders above the rest – magical.'

As Philippe drank water and joked with his teammates, the youth coach went to speak to José Carlos.

'Your son is the best player I've seen in a very long time,' he said. 'Maybe ever!'

Philippe's dad smiled. 'Thanks, I'm glad that you were impressed. So do you think he's good enough for the Vasco academy?'

The youth coach laughed. 'Good enough? He's probably *too* good! I'd like him to come for a trial and see how he likes it. Does that sound okay?'

José Carlos called Philippe over and the youth coach repeated his offer.

'What do you think?' his dad asked him.

Philippe was very shy but he couldn't hide his big smile. A trial at Vasco da Gama – this was the best news ever. Cristiano and Leandro would be so jealous when he told them.

'Yes please!' he told the youth coach.

## CHAPTER 5

# VASCO DA GAMA

'How are you feeling?' José Carlos asked as they drove to the trial.

Philippe nodded and stared out of the car window. The truth was that he was too nervous to even speak. Until now, he had only played fun football with his brothers, and then *futsal* with his friends. This was serious – proper, real football for a proper, big club. Philippe was scared that people would see that he didn't know what he was doing.

'Just do your best today, kiddo,' his dad continued. 'There's no pressure at all. If you have fun out there, that's great. But if you don't, you've tried and that's great too. What is it I always say to you guys?'

'Be brave and try new things,' they said together.

The problem was that Philippe really hated new things. He was shy and he found it hard to be the new kid who didn't know anyone else. But he couldn't back out now – they had arrived at the Vasco da Gama youth training ground.

'Ready to show them what you've got?' José Carlos asked with a smile.

Philippe nodded. His heart was beating so fast that he felt it might burst out of his chest. He could see the other boys warming up on the pitch, laughing and joking with each other because they had been playing together for years. Philippe was the odd one out.

'Deep breath,' his dad said, and they took one together.

The Vasco coach was there at the entrance to welcome them. He handed Philippe a black and white club shirt and told him to go and get warmed up.

'Good luck!' his dad said. 'I'll be right here in the stands, watching and cheering.'

José Carlos was just as nervous as his son. He knew that Philippe had lots of talent but what if he wasn't ready for this yet? He was only eight years old. If the trial went badly, it might put him off playing football forever. He just wanted his son to enjoy himself.

Philippe ran onto the pitch and joined the other boys. As they all shook hands with him, his whole body was shaking. Once that was done, the boys went back to their conversation, which he wasn't part of. Philippe felt like he had made a big mistake. What was he doing? He didn't want to be there.

Just as José Carlos took his seat in the stands, he saw his son running back off the field. 'Perhaps he needs the toilet,' he thought at first but no, that wasn't where he was going. He was running to his dad.

'What's wrong, kiddo?' he asked, but Philippe just burst into tears. Once he had calmed down, José Carlos tried again.

'I don't want to be the new kid,' Philippe cried. 'They're all so much better than me! I just want to go back and play with my friends.'

'How do you know they're so much better than you?' his dad asked. 'You haven't even seen them play yet. I know it's scary but I want you to give it another go. If you hate it, we'll never come back, I promise! Be brave.'

Philippe watched the boys on the pitch. They were kicking a ball around and doing cool tricks. It did look like fun. Once he felt calmer, they walked down to the touchline together. The coach was waiting for him to start the session.

'Okay Dad, I'll give it another go,' Philippe decided.

'Good boy, I'm proud of you!'

The first touch of the football was all it took. The nerves and shyness just disappeared. Philippe was in his element, passing in triangles and dribbling between cones.

'Excellent!' the coach clapped.

José Carlos relaxed too. He could tell that his son was having fun. Philippe was even laughing with his new teammates.

'I knew he'd thank me later,' he said to himself.

In the seven-a-side match, Philippe worked hard to create chances for his team. He didn't score himself but he set up two goals for the strikers with his dribbling skills. At the end, he was exhausted but still buzzing.

'Do you think I did okay?' Philippe asked his dad.

'You were brilliant!' José Carlos replied. 'But more importantly, did you enjoy the training?'

'Yeah, it was awesome!'

'So, you'd like to come back next week?'

'Yes please!'

Soon the trial period was over and Philippe was asked to become a proper Vasco youth team player. It was a question with a very easy answer – yes!

The coach was delighted. 'I knew as soon as I saw him play *futsal*,' he told Philippe's dad. 'This kid's got something really special. He might be quiet off the pitch but, on it, he's bold and brave. And he understands the game in a way that's impossible to teach. Somehow, he just *knows* it!'

It didn't take long for Philippe to become Vasco's star player. He learned to dribble less and look up more to find that killer pass. With the ball at his feet, he could think faster than the other boys. He saw runs that the defenders couldn't see. It was a rare gift. As he moved from the Under-9s to the Under-10s to the Under-11s, Philippe got better and better. Word started spreading.

'Wow, who's that wonderkid?' people asked.

'That's the Little Magician.'

## CHAPTER 6

# RONALDINHO

'Ronaldinho gets the ball on the left and dribbles at Cristiano. One stepover, then another, then another – he's making the defender look like a fool! With a perfect rainbow flick, he's through on goal... as the goalkeeper comes out, Ronaldinho fakes to shoot left but shoots bottom right instead. He scores with a brilliant no-look finish!'

Leandro put down his pretend microphone and ran on to the pitch. He replaced Cristiano, who was exhausted after being humiliated by his youngest brother.

'Get tight on him. Kick him if you have to!' Cristiano told Leandro as he walked off.

Just because Philippe was now playing for the Vasco da Gama youth team, it didn't mean that their local matches had to stop. Actually, it just made them even more competitive.

'Come on, that's a foul!' Philippe shouted as he lay on the floor and wiped the blood off his scraped knee. Six years had passed since that first game but nothing had changed between the brothers.

'What's the referee's decision?' Leandro asked, looking at Cristiano.

It was time for him to get his own back on Philippe. 'No, you've got to be stronger there, "Ronaldinho". Play on!'

Ronaldinho was Brazil's number one superstar and Philippe's favourite player. There were many reasons to love Ronaldinho. When he got the ball, he always looked to attack and to create chances. He scored brilliant goals and he set up lots more with his dribbling. He was full of energy and full of tricks. But as well as being an amazing footballer, Ronaldinho was also a born entertainer. He never stopped dancing, laughing and smiling. Philippe loved his samba spirit.

'When I'm older, I want to be just like him!' he told his brothers.

When Brazil competed in the 2002 World Cup in South Korea and Japan, the Coutinho family watched all of their matches on TV. Cristiano loved Ronaldo, Leandro loved Rivaldo and Philippe loved Ronaldinho. He would never forget Ronaldinho's incredible goal against England in the quarter-finals in Fukuroi, Japan. The score was 1-1 and Brazil won a free-kick wide on the right, 35 yards from goal. No-one thought that Ronaldinho would shoot, least of all the England goalkeeper David Seaman.

When he came forward off his line, Ronaldinho spotted it straight away. There wasn't much space behind the keeper but he was bold and talented enough to lob him. The ball sailed over Seaman's head and into the top corner.

*Goooooooooooooooooooooooaaaaaaaaaaaaaaaaaaaaall llllllllllllllllllll!!!!!!!!!!!!!!!!*

As Ronaldinho celebrated on the pitch in Japan, Philippe celebrated in their living room in Brazil. He jumped up and down on the sofa, shouting until his throat got sore.

'That was such a clever strike!' he cheered.

'I'm not sure he meant to do that,' Leandro said, trying to wind his brother up. 'I think that was a cross that went wrong.'

His wind-up worked. Philippe looked furious. 'Don't be stupid! Ronaldinho knew exactly what he was doing. He's a genius!'

The next day, on the concrete pitch by their house, Philippe practised 'the Ronaldinho' again and again. He even copied his fast run-up. It was very difficult to side-foot the ball with so much power and curl but, eventually, Philippe was finding the top corner every time. Now he just needed a goalkeeper.

'Leandro!' Philippe called across the street. 'Can you come and be Seaman for a bit?'

His brother stood a little off his line and waited for the free-kick. As the ball came towards him, he made an easy save.

'You need to get more dip on the shot!' Leandro suggested.

Philippe tried again. And again and again. After ten attempts, the ball finally went over Leandro's head and came back down in time to land in the top corner.

'Yesssssssssssssssssssssssssss!' Philippe shouted. He copied Ronaldinho's goal celebration, grabbing his T-shirt like it was the yellow Brazil shirt and shaking it at the non-existent crowd. All the hard work was worth it.

'Just you wait until I get an opportunity to lob the keeper in a match,' he told his brother excitedly as they walked back home. 'I'm going to score a "Ronaldinho"!'

Philippe didn't get the chance to watch many of his hero's matches for Barcelona, but he watched videos of them on the Internet every week. Philippe's favourite was Ronaldinho's first goal for the club, against Sevilla. As he dribbled forward from the halfway line, he beat one defender and then nutmegged another. He shot from 30 yards out and the ball rocketed in off the crossbar.

'*Golazo*!!!' the Spanish commentators screamed.

Philippe watched that video hundreds of times. And then he went on to the concrete pitch and practised it. When he felt confident, he called his family over.

'Leandro, you start from there and, Cristiano, you start from there,' Philippe said, putting his defenders in the right places. Everything had to be perfect. 'Dad, you're in goal!'

It took a long time but Philippe got there eventually. At full speed, he dribbled past one brother, then the other, and hit a thunderous shot into the net.

'Great – can we go now?' Leandro asked. They had been doing it for over an hour and he was bored.

But Philippe wasn't satisfied. 'What's wrong?' his dad asked.

'The shot was meant to go in off the crossbar,' he replied. 'That's what he did in the video.'

José Carlos laughed. 'Sorry, your shot was too good for that. Do you know what this means, though? You're now officially better than Ronaldinho!'

## CHAPTER 7

# PHILIPPE AND NEYMAR

Philippe was improving every week. Soon he was named as the captain of Vasco da Gama's Under-14s team. He was still a very shy person, so he didn't lead by shouting and organising his teammates. He let his friend Souza do that from defensive midfield. Instead, Philippe led by creating and scoring goals.

'Get the ball to Phil!' the coach shouted if they were ever not winning. 'He knows what to do with it!'

Some players panicked on the ball, or tried to show off every trick in the book. But Philippe was calm and clever. He was learning when to use his amazing skills, when to pass, and when to shoot. He made everything look so easy.

'Phil to the rescue again!' Souza shouted as his teammate scored another winning goal.

But the more magic Philippe performed, the more everyone expected of him. Brazilians were always talking about the country's best players for the future. Every year, there were new stars. The local people were already calling Philippe 'the next big thing'.

'I'm only thirteen!' he tried to explain but no-one seemed to listen.

'When Ronaldinho was thirteen, he scored 23 goals in a 23-0 win!'

'Yes but I'm not Ronaldinho!'

Philippe was wasting his breath.

There was a fierce rivalry between Brazil's two biggest cities, Rio de Janeiro and São Paulo. They were always competing over who could produce the best footballers. Ronaldo was from Rio, whereas Cafu was from São Paulo. At Under-14s level, Philippe was the star in Rio and a brilliant young striker called Neymar was the star in São Paulo.

'Neymar certainly scores more goals – have you seen his record? It's unbelievable!'

'Philippe is less selfish, though. He's more of a playmaker and he sets up a lot more goals than Neymar does.'

The debate went on and on. And it only got worse when Philippe's Vasco played Neymar's Santos. Philippe was looking forward to the challenge of competing against the top talent, but he tried to ignore what the fans were saying.

'It's not like it's a one-on-one match!' he said to his brothers. 'I've got teammates and so does Neymar. So why are we the only players that anyone talks about?'

He didn't get any sympathy from Leandro. 'Sorry superstar, that's just the way it is!'

But he did get some good advice from Cristiano. 'Just focus on playing the same way you play in every other match. Remember to trust your teammates to help you. Be the leader, not the show-off.'

Neymar was a bit taller than Philippe but he didn't look any stronger. Philippe had seen videos of Neymar's skills. He was an excellent player but so was Philippe. They could inspire each other to become even better. Before kick-off, they shook hands and laughed about the rivalry.

'It's so ridiculous!' Philippe said. 'They should just be happy that we're both Brazilians. Good luck today.'

'May the best boy win!' Neymar joked.

The match lived up to all the hype. As soon as the game started, it was non-stop, entertaining, end-to-end football. It was like they were back on the *futsal* court. Philippe did something special and then so did Neymar; Vasco put together a great team move and then so did Santos.

'What a match!' Neymar said to Philippe at the end. They were both so exhausted that they could barely speak. They stood chatting for a while, remembering the best bits of the game.

'That third goal you scored was unreal! To try that flick when there were three defenders in front of you – that was genius right there!'

'What about that no-look pass to set up the fourth goal? You had our whole defence on a piece of string. *That* was genius right there!'

They swapped shirts and phone numbers. It was the start of a great friendship.

'It would be so cool if we could play on the same team next time,' Neymar added with a big grin on his face. 'We're made to play together!'

'For Brazil!' they cheered together.

Until then, Philippe had always thought of football as fun. His parents wanted him to get a good education so that he could get a good job. But what if football could be his job? He knew that the top superstars earned lots of money doing what they loved. That sounded like the best job in the world!

Playing with Neymar, Philippe believed that he could become a superstar too. He had the talent to win lots of trophies for his country and for the biggest clubs in Europe. It was a dream but suddenly it felt possible.

'Dad, do you think I could become a professional footballer one day?' Philippe asked as they drove home.

José Carlos smiled. He had been waiting for that question. 'One step at a time, kiddo. If you carry on developing like this, there's no reason why not. You're a natural – anyone can see that. Keep doing your best and let's see what happens next!'

What happened next was Philippe was selected to play for Brazil's Under-14s team. It was the proudest moment of his life when his dad got off the phone and told him the news.

'I'm going to play for the national team!' Philippe cheered again and again as he ran around the house with his T-shirt over his head.

When he arrived for the match, Philippe went straight to the changing rooms. He was shy and needed his friend's support. Finally, a boy burst through the door, dancing to the music blaring out of his headphones.

'Let's do this!' Neymar shouted, giving him a big hug.

'Awesome – I can't wait to play together!'

'For Brazil!' they both cheered.

## CHAPTER 8

# AINE

Philippe didn't really like going to parties. He loved
hanging out with his friends and Vasco teammates,
but standing in a big room with lots and lots of
people? Having awkward chats with total strangers?
No thanks – that was his idea of a nightmare.

'Are you sure about this?' Philippe asked Dani
on the way to the party. 'We could just play football
instead!'

His friend shook his head and rolled his eyes.
'Come on, we do that every day! Fabio says that the
music will be banging and, more importantly, he's
invited lots of girls!'

Philippe nodded and followed Dani into the party.

He wasn't going to abandon his friend but he also wasn't going to enjoy himself. He never did when it came to girls. He found it really hard to talk to any new person but, if it was an attractive girl, he got totally tongue-tied.

'Hey, I just spotted someone I know,' Dani shouted over the loud stereo. 'I'm going over to say hi. I'll be back in a bit.'

'Brilliant,' Philippe thought to himself sarcastically. He had been left on his own already. He looked around but he couldn't see anyone that he recognised. He stood in the corner and waited for Dani to return.

'Cool party, right?' Philippe heard a female voice say nearby.

He looked up and panicked for two reasons: 1) the girl was very beautiful, and 2) she was talking to *him*! This was when everything usually went wrong for him – he would go bright red, start sweating and say stupid, boring things. Philippe took a deep breath and tried his best.

'Yeah, great tunes!' he said. A good, smooth start.

'Nice to meet you, I'm Philippe.'

'And I'm Aine,' she said, flashing a lovely smile. 'So how do you know Fabio?'

'We go to school together,' he said, trying to sound casual. 'How about you?'

'We're old family friends,' Aine explained. 'When we were babies, our parents made us take baths together!'

Philippe laughed. 'Poor you!'

Aine was laughing too. 'Yeah, Fabio was a real bully back then! When the adults weren't looking, he would splash water in my face and pull my hair.'

Philippe was starting to relax and enjoy himself. 'It doesn't sound like he's changed much since then!' he joked.

Aine laughed again and this time for longer. Philippe was talking to an attractive girl and he was entertaining her! It was a miracle. But Dani was walking across the room towards them. His friend was definitely going to ruin everything.

'Dani, this is Aine,' Philippe said. 'She's a friend of Fabio's family.'

'Cool, are you from round here?' Dani asked.

'Yeah, I've lived in this neighbourhood all my life.'

'Me too,' Philippe said. 'I can't believe we've never met before!'

'Maybe we have and you just don't know it!' Aine teased.

Dani quickly got the message that he wasn't wanted. 'I'm going to leave you and the football star to it,' he said, winking at his friend before moving on.

'So you're a footballer?' Aine asked.

Now Philippe was feeling embarrassed. 'Y-yeah, I play football.'

'Who do you play for?'

'Vasco,' he replied. He didn't want to tell her that he also played for the Brazil Under-15s.

Aine smiled. 'That's really cool! Why are you so shy about it?'

Philippe shrugged. 'I just don't really like talking about myself.'

'Okay, well I won't ask you any more questions... today!'

For the rest of the party, he asked Aine questions

about her life. He was having such a good time that he didn't want it to end. It was the first time that had ever happened.

'Come on Phil, we've gotta go now,' Dani called out.

Philippe turned back to Aine. 'It was really nice to meet you...' he began.

Luckily, Aine knew what he was trying to say. 'Yes, we should hang out soon. Here's my phone number.'

Philippe couldn't stop smiling as he walked home with Dani.

'So was she really impressed when you told her that you're going to be a footballer and earn lots and lots of money?' Dani asked.

'Don't jinx me!' Philippe said. 'No, we actually didn't really talk about football.'

'You, not talking about football?'

'I know, weird, right? But I liked it.'

Over the next few months, Philippe and Aine spent lots of time together. They watched films and met each other's families and friends. Family meant to a lot to both of them. That was one of the big things that they had in common. Their relationship seemed to be going really well, or at least that's what Philippe thought.

'We've been hanging out a lot recently...' Aine said one day as they sat drinking coffee.

'Yes?' he replied, looking confused.

She laughed. 'Wow, sometimes you really are clueless! Well if you're too shy to ask me, I'll have to ask you. Philippe, will you be my boyfriend?'

He felt very embarrassed but, at the same time, he couldn't help laughing. Aine was definitely the right girl for him. 'Of course!' he said eventually, with a kiss.

# CHAPTER 9

# INTER MILAN

Inter Milan had lots of scouts in South America. The Italian club was always looking for the best new talent in countries like Argentina, Uruguay and Brazil. They wanted to find 'the next Ronaldo' or 'the next Ronaldinho' before anyone else did.

However, Inter weren't the only ones watching Philippe. All of the top European teams were interested in signing him and he hadn't even made his professional debut yet. Scouts called his dad to offer him money, a job and a house.

'You just focus on enjoying your football,' José Carlos told his son. 'I'll deal with all these crazy clubs!'

Vasco da Gama tried to calm things down but there wasn't much that they could do. They had seen this situation so many times before. Once rich clubs like Inter Milan and Real Madrid wanted a player, they paid as much as it took to get him.

The interest had started when Philippe was picked for the Brazil Under-14s with Neymar. But it really increased when he joined the Vasco Under-17s squad. The coach, Rodney Goncalves, had been keeping an eye on Philippe for years. He could see the star talent but he didn't want to rush things.

Vasco were winning their match 2-0. With ten minutes to go, Goncalves decided that it was time to bring on fresh legs. As he turned around to look at his substitutes, Philippe was the first one he saw. That was because he was so eager to play that he couldn't sit still on the bench.

'Why not?' Goncalves thought to himself. 'He's young but he needs the experience.'

As soon as Philippe came on, the game changed. Before that, it had been a difficult game for Vasco but suddenly, he made it look so easy. The ball stayed stuck to his foot, no matter how quickly he ran or how suddenly he turned. And if he didn't already have the ball, Philippe was running into space and calling for it.

'Nice play, Phil!' Goncalves called out. He could hear the excitement growing around him. Were scouts already watching this kid? If not, they soon would be. He was a little magician.

The match finished 5-0. Philippe scored two great goals and he set up the other with an amazing dribble. He had done all that in only ten minutes. So what would he do in a full match? Goncalves couldn't wait to find out.

Most young players needed time to get used to Under-17s football but not Philippe. He could think faster than the other boys and he could see passes and spaces that they couldn't.

'He won't be here long,' Goncalves thought to himself sadly. The best Brazilian kids always moved to Europe eventually.

He was right. After dinner one night, José Carlos gave Philippe a decision to make. 'Son, Inter Milan would like you to go to Italy for a visit. What do you think?'

Inter Milan! Philippe didn't need to think about it. It was Ronaldo's old club and now they had superstars like Luis Figo, Zlatan Ibrahimovič and Hernán Crespo. 'Of course I'll go!' he told his dad.

Philippe was so excited. He couldn't wait to tell Aine and his friends about this. He was going to train with the Italian champions. But then he had a scary flashback to the awful start of his trial at Vasco when he was eight. 'Wait, you're coming with me, right?'

José Carlos laughed. Sometimes he forgot that his son was still a child. 'Of course I'll come!' he echoed.

When they arrived in Milan, one of the Inter coaches took them to the club's training ground. Philippe couldn't believe what he saw. The place was so big that it looked like a city.

'Olà!' a voice said behind them.

Philippe turned around; it was José Mourinho, the Inter manager! He was still a shy boy but now he was also star-struck. He was really glad that his dad was there to do the talking for him.

Mourinho took them on a tour of the facilities. Philippe had been worried about not being able to understand people in Italy but it was okay because Mourinho spoke Portuguese like he did. Mourinho was very friendly and he had big plans for Philippe.

'We have lots of great players here but what we're missing is a world-class playmaker,' the manager said. 'We defend well and we score goals but we need more magic in midfield. That's where you come into it!'

For Philippe, it all felt like a dream. After talking to Mourinho, he went to train with the first team. He was playing football with Figo, Zlatan and Crespo! He couldn't wait to tell Souza about it.

'Nice to meet you, kid!' Maxwell, a Brazilian defender, said with a smile. It was helpful that lots of the players spoke Portuguese too, but Philippe could only smile in reply. He had never been so nervous on the football pitch.

However, he couldn't let that stop him from showing his talent. 'I'm good enough to be here,' he kept saying to himself. As always, it only took a few touches of the ball before Philippe started to enjoy himself. He was confident on the dribble and brave in the tackle. He wanted them to see that although he was a skilful player, he could work hard too.

After two days, Inter were impressed with Philippe, and Philippe was impressed with Inter.

'I really want to play here!' he told his dad. He needed to speak to Aine first but how could he say no to working with Mourinho?

Soon, the deal was done. Philippe would be an Inter Milan player but not quite yet. The clubs had agreed that he would stay at Vasco for a little longer before moving to Italy.

'Keep developing your skills and we'll see you back here in two years!' Mourinho told Philippe as they said their goodbyes.

## CHAPTER 10

# PROMOTION

Philippe was relieved to be staying in Brazil for another two years. He wasn't yet ready to leave his friends behind to go on his big, scary European adventure. First, he wanted to get some experience of professional football. And, hopefully, become a local hero.

Vasco da Gama had just been relegated to Série B for the first time in ninety-four years. It was an absolute disaster but the club hoped to bounce straight back up to Série A. At seventeen years old, Philippe was ready to play his part.

'I'm not scared!' he told the new coach, Dorival Júnior.

Dorival looked at the small, curly-haired boy in front of him and laughed. He knew that Philippe had incredible skills but could he really handle the big Brazilian defenders? There was only one way to find out. 'You should be scared!' he warned.

Philippe made his debut as a second-half substitute. He couldn't wait to show off his skills in front of the home fans. They had been hearing about him for years. Finally, they would see Vasco's 'next big thing' in action.

Philippe's first touch was a short pass and his teammate passed back to him. With his second and third touches, Philippe dribbled at the full-back. As he dropped the shoulder and cut inside, the defender hacked him down. Foul!

'Get up, little superstar!' the defender called out. 'Don't ever think you're too good for us because we'll bring you right back down to earth.'

'Are you okay?' his teammate Élton said, helping him up. 'You better get used to that kind of treatment!'

Philippe pulled up his socks and kept attacking.

It was like playing at their local concrete pitch all over again. He wasn't going to let a few dirty tackles stop him. The next time, he used his speed to escape down the wing and crossed the ball into Élton. On the sidelines, Dorival clapped.

'The kid's got spirit!' he thought to himself.

At first, the same things happened again and again.

Philippe rolled the ball across with his right foot, then dragged it back with his left. The defender kicked his leg. Foul!

Philippe twisted and turned, one way and then the other and then the other again. The defender tried to focus on the ball but it was making him feel dizzy. In the end, he just pushed Phillipe to the floor. Foul!

Philippe flicked the ball over the defender's head and as he ran to control it, the defender tripped him up. Foul!

But after a lot of bumps and bruises, Philippe learned to avoid the fouls. He used his quick feet and balance to jump, dodge and swerve. And with Dorival's guidance, he spent less time dribbling and more time looking for the pass.

'Even you can't beat a whole team on your own!' his manager kept telling him. 'If you try, you'll lose the ball every time.'

Philippe was improving with every minute on the pitch. He was playing with confidence and intelligence. By looking up more often, he could spot his teammates' runs and play clever passes for them to score. An assist felt nearly as good as a goal.

Only nearly, though. When a defender intercepted a through-ball in the penalty area, Philippe was there in a flash. He was desperate to get his first Vasco goal. Some young players might have passed, or gone for accuracy over power. But not Philippe. He struck the ball as powerfully as he could. It flew into the top corner before the goalkeeper even saw it.

*Goooooooooooooooooaaaaaaaaaaaaaaaaaaaaalllllllll lllllllllllllllllllllllll!!!!!!!!!!!!*

Philippe fell to his knees and pointed to the sky. What a special moment. He would never forget his first goal for his hometown club. As his teammates hugged him, he could hear the Vasco supporters chanting his name:

*Coutinho! Coutinho! Coutinho!*

He could feel the goosebumps spreading across his skin, and the tears forming in his eyes. This had been Philippe's dream since he first kicked a football; this was what all of the hard work had been about. He was a star player for his favourite club and the fans loved him. Youngsters were already wearing his name on the back of their shirts. It was crazy but amazing.

Philippe was still a youngster himself. He still looked up to his heroes, especially Ronaldinho. One day, he got a call from his agent.

'Phil, what are you doing on Wednesday night?' he asked.

'Nothing, why?'

'Ronaldinho wants you to play in his charity football match.'

Philippe's heart started beating really fast. Was this a joke? It had to be. 'Are you sure?'

His agent laughed. 'Yes, I promise I'm not winding you up!'

Philippe was very nervous about meeting his idol. What should he say? He wanted to seem like a professional footballer, not a little kid wanting an autograph.

'Welcome, thanks for playing!' Ronaldinho said, flashing that big, toothy smile.

Once he saw that, Philippe relaxed. Soon they were chatting happily about the Brazilian league and their favourite players.

'I have a question for you,' Philippe said eventually, plucking up the courage. 'You know that free-kick you scored against England at the 2002 World Cup? My brother always said that you meant to cross the ball instead but I'm sure you meant to shoot. I'm right, aren't I?'

Ronaldinho's smile grew even wider. 'Of course I meant to shoot!'

Playing with his hero was one of the best experiences of Philippe's life. He was really living the dream now but, luckily, his brothers were there to keep his feet firmly on the ground. They were both lawyers now, so it was their job to argue.

'After that performance, I don't think Ronnie will be asking you to play again next year!' Cristiano teased. 'How did you miss that chance? It was an open goal!'

When Philippe told Leandro about his free-kick conversation with Ronaldinho, his brother just shook his head. 'No, I still don't believe him!'

Vasco da Gama won the Série B title with ease. Philippe was so pleased to have the winner's medal around his neck and then later, the trophy in his hands. He jumped up and down with his teammates and sang all the Vasco songs.

'I'll miss you!' Souza shouted. He was also going to Europe, but to play for Porto.

Philippe was delighted with his first season of professional football but it was time to move on. Now that he was 18 years old, Inter Milan wanted him to join the squad. Hopefully, he would keep on developing his skills in Italy.

He would really miss Brazil and especially Vasco. He had played there for eleven years, from the age of seven. The club meant so much to him and his family. Promotion was the perfect way to say goodbye.

## CHAPTER 11

# LEARNING FROM THE LOWS

Meanwhile, Philippe's international career continued to flourish. 2009 was a big year for Brazil's Under-17 team. First, they played in the South American Championships in Chile where, if they did well, they would play in the FIFA Under-17 World Cup in Nigeria. They were one of the favourites to win both tournaments. Many of Philippe's teammates were desperate to impress the scouts from top European clubs, but he had already done that.

'I just want to enjoy myself and do my best for Brazil,' Philippe told his dad.

'Absolutely!' José Carlos replied. He was very proud of his son's mature attitude. Despite the great expectations, Philippe was staying calm and focused. That was a very good sign for his future.

Only four South American teams would make it through to the Under-17 World Cup, and they would be decided in the South American Under-17 Championship, where Brazil were in Group A with Colombia, and their biggest rivals Argentina and Uruguay were in Group B.

'If we top the group, we're on our way to Nigeria!' the coach Luiz Antonio Nizzo (aka Lucho) explained to the players before the competition began.

Philippe had been looking forward to terrorising defences with Neymar again, but unfortunately his friend had to miss the tournament. Without him, Philippe was definitely Brazil's best player. They were relying on his magic.

Philippe didn't let his country down. Not only did he create lots of goals with his clever dribbling and passing, but he also scored two penalties in their comfortable wins over Paraguay and Peru. He was enjoying himself, just like he had promised his dad. Three wins and one defeat was enough to give Brazil the top spot.

'Africa, here we come!' he shouted as he jumped up and down with his teammate Casemiro.

But before that, they still had one more game to go: the South American final. Brazil had beaten Argentina in 2005 and 2007, but could they get the hat-trick? It was up to Philippe and his teammates.

In a very exciting game, Brazil went 2-0 up, with Philippe scoring the brilliant second goal. It looked like they had won the final, but Argentina fought back to 2-2. In the penalty shoot-out, Philippe felt confident. He was Brazil's first-choice taker and he had scored two already in the tournament. He stepped up and... missed!

'Nooooooo!' Philippe screamed up into the sky. As he walked back to the halfway line, he stared down at the ground. His team had been counting on him.

'Don't worry!' Wellington said, putting an arm around his shoulder. 'We'll still win this.'

Wellington was right. He scored the winning penalty and Brazil were the Under-17 South American champions again. Philippe was so relieved that he cried tears of joy. When it was his turn to hold the trophy, he didn't want to ever let go of it.

'Congratulations!' Neymar cheered when he next saw Philippe. 'I can't wait for us to play at the World Cup together.'

That had been their dream for years; to become the deadly duo who led their nation to glory. In Nigeria, that dream could become a reality. It wouldn't be easy but Philippe and Neymar were full of self-belief.

In the first match against Japan, Brazil looked dangerous every time they got the ball. But when they lost the ball, they didn't defend well at all. After sixty-five minutes, they were drawing. Philippe picked the ball up in the middle, turned and looked for Neymar. They had practised this so many times. Neymar ran between the centre-backs and Philippe delivered the perfect pass on a plate.

As the goalkeeper ran out to close him down, Neymar tapped the ball round him and then collected his own pass. 2-1! Philippe jumped into Neymar's arms. The deadly duo had come to Brazil's rescue.

'When we play like that, no-one can stop us!' Neymar shouted.

But in the next game, against Mexico, they didn't play like that. The Mexican defence was so strong that Philippe and Neymar hardly ever got past them. And when they did, they tried too hard to score the perfect goal. All of their flicks and tricks came to nothing.

'Slow it down, make it simple!' Casemiro shouted from midfield.

In the first half, Philippe hit a shot from outside the penalty area but it flew high over the crossbar. In the second half, Philippe hit a much better long-range shot but this time, the goalkeeper made a spectacular save. A few minutes later, Mexico scored the winning goal. The Brazilian players left the pitch in shock. They now had to beat Switzerland to keep their World Cup hopes alive.

Ahead of the big match, the coach Lucho had a word with Philippe and Neymar. 'I love the way you play together but sometimes, we just need to score!' the coach told them. 'The fast dribbling, the one-twos – when it all works, it's magical. But when it doesn't quite work, you need to find less beautiful ways to get the ball in the net.'

They listened carefully to Lucho's instructions. A simple tap-in was worth the same as a stunning strike. 'A goal's a goal,' Philippe and Neymar reminded each other before kick-off.

Unfortunately, Switzerland took the lead after twenty minutes. Philippe tried and tried but he couldn't quite create the equaliser. Neither could Neymar. The ball just wouldn't cross the goal-line. At the final whistle, the Brazilian players trudged off the pitch in silence. They had failed.

It was the first big setback of Philippe's football career. It hurt but it also made him stronger. He loved winning all the time but at some point, he needed to learn to lose. That was a very important lesson in becoming a better player and a better person.

'We'll have plenty more chances,' Neymar reassured him, once the disappointment had started to fade. 'First there's the Under-20 World Cup and then if we're lucky, we might get to play in three or four *proper* World Cups too!'

## CHAPTER 12

# THE ITALIAN JOB

'This kid is the future of Inter!' the club chairman, Massimo Moratti, happily told the Italian media.

Philippe smiled as he held up the blue and black shirt with his name on the back. But the last thing he needed was extra pressure. He was only eighteen years old and he had just arrived in a foreign country. In 2010, two years after signing the contract, he had finally made the move from Vasco de Gama to Inter Milan. In the meantime, Mourinho had unfortunately left to join Real Madrid, and former Liverpool manager Rafa Benitez was now in charge.

'Don't listen to him – Morrati is just getting

over-excited,' Benitez reassured him. 'Take your time to settle in.'

But Philippe found the culture shock very difficult. The club tried their best to make him feel at home. He had three friendly Brazilian teammates – goalkeeper Júlio César and defenders Maicon and Lúcio – and his parents and Aine had come to Italy with him. But that didn't stop Philippe feeling homesick.

'I walk down the street and I can't understand a single word of what people are saying!' he complained to Aine.

'Neither can I!' his girlfriend replied with a comforting smile. She was still only seventeen and she had come all the way from Brazil to support Philippe.

'When the coaches talk, Lúcio and Maicon translate most of the words for me,' he admitted, 'but I'm too shy to tell them that I still don't understand the instructions.'

'Don't worry, if we study hard, we'll be fluent in Italian in no time,' Aine encouraged him.

It got even harder when his parents went back to Brazil but Philippe never gave up on achieving his dream. On the football pitch, his Inter career got off to a good start. In his second preseason friendly in Canada, Maicon passed the ball to him on the left side of the penalty area. Philippe controlled the ball with his right foot and smashed it into the net with his left.

*Goooooooooooooooooooaaaaaaaaaaaaaaaaaallllllllll llllllllllllllll!!!!!!!!!!!!!!!!!*

Philippe felt a mix of joy and relief at scoring his first goal for the club. He punched his fist and then looked to his Brazilian teammate. Maicon gave him a thumbs-up, so he gave Maicon a thumbs-up back. He was one of the Inter guys now.

When he got to play football and score goals, Philippe was happy. When he had to do strength training in the gym instead, he wasn't happy at all. But the Inter coaches gave him no choice.

'You need to build up your strength before you play against the defenders in Serie A,' they warned him. 'If you don't, they'll push you off the ball every time.'

Back in Brazil, no-one had really worried about his size. With magical skills like his, it didn't matter that he wasn't very big. In fact, being small made Philippe more agile. He could skip away from crunching tackles.

'A bit more power in your legs is no bad thing,' his teammate Christian Chivu told him. 'Trust me – I'm one of those Serie A defenders that they're talking about!'

Philippe started the season on the bench. He didn't mind because he was still very young and he was still learning about Italian football. For the first time, Philippe had to think about defending and marking.

'In Serie A, an attacker doesn't just attack,' Goran Pandev explained. 'We have to help the team too.'

Philippe listened to all of the advice but as the weeks went by, he wasn't getting any closer to the starting line-up.

'I play ten minutes one week and then six the next,' he complained to his mum on the phone. 'What am I supposed to do in that time?'

As usual, 'patience' was Esmerelda's wise answer for her son.

Finally, Philippe's big chance came in the Champions League match against Tottenham. On the left wing, his job was to create chances for Inter's superstar striker Samuel Eto'o. Philippe couldn't wait to play from the start.

After two minutes, he dribbled infield and passed to Samuel. Samuel passed to captain Javier Zanetti and he scored. 1-0! As they celebrated the goal, Javier Zanetti gave Philippe a high-five. 'Great work!' he cheered.

That gave Philippe lots of confidence. When Javier passed to him, he turned and dribbled towards goal. Philippe spotted Samuel's run between the centre-backs and played a perfect through-ball. Samuel scored to make it 4-0. It wasn't even half-time yet.

'Great work!' Samuel said as they hugged.

Philippe was doing so well that Benitez let him play the full ninety minutes. At the final whistle, everyone was talking about Tottenham's Gareth Bale, who had scored a hat-trick in the second half. But Christian was full of praise for Philippe.

'What a performance!' he shouted as they returned to the dressing room. 'We've all seen what you can do in training and now you're doing it in actual matches. Keep going!'

But unfortunately, Philippe couldn't keep going. First, he suffered a knee injury and then in December 2010, Benitez was sacked after just six months as manager. The new manager, Leonardo, didn't want Philippe in his starting line-up, and so he was back on the bench again.

In March 2011, Inter were losing 3-1 to Bayern Munich in the Champions League Round of 16. After fifty minutes, Leonardo sent Philippe on to replace Dejan Stankovi .

'They're thrashing us – we need your magic!' his manager told him.

When Philippe got the ball, he cut inside and played a killer pass across to Samuel. He set up Wesley Sneijder to score. 3-2!

After that, they missed chance after chance. But

eventually, Goran Pandev got the crucial goal. Inter were 3-3 on aggregate but were going through on away goals.

At the final whistle, Leonardo ran over and hugged Philippe.

'What a difference you made!' he shouted excitedly.

Philippe smiled widely. It was another high in a largely frustrating first season in European football – and there was time for just one more. Leonardo named him in the starting line-up for the Serie A match against Fiorentina in May.

In front of the home San Siro crowd, Philippe was determined to shine. They hadn't seen him at his entertaining best yet. He was instrumental in setting up three good attempts at goal in the first half with his quick feet and quick thinking. Philippe was definitely Inter's danger man.

In the second half and with fifteen minutes to go, Inter won a free-kick. Samuel had been substituted, so it was Philippe's turn to take it. He looked up and saw that the goalkeeper was standing to one side of his goal. If Philippe could hit the ball into the other corner with enough power, dip and accuracy, he would definitely score. That's exactly what he did. The goalkeeper stretched his arm out as far as he could, but he couldn't reach it.

*Goooooooooooooooooooooaaaaaaaaaaaaaaaaaallllll lllllllllllllllllllllllllllllll!!!!!!!!!!!*

Philippe finally had his first official goal for Inter, and what a strike it was. He ran towards the fans with a massive grin on his face. He drew a heart in the air and blew kisses to all of them. They had been very kind and supportive towards him.

'What a year!' Philippe laughed afterwards, while enjoying a short holiday with Aine. 'Maybe Italy isn't so bad after all!'

## CHAPTER 13

# WORLD CHAMPION

Wherever Neymar went, Philippe was never far behind. Neymar made his senior Brazil debut in August 2010 and, two months later, Mano Menezes included Philippe in the national squad for a friendly match against Iran.

'Great news – we'll be playing together again in Abu Dhabi!' Philippe told Neymar excitedly on the phone.

But this time, his friend wasn't picked for the squad. 'Congrats and good luck!' Neymar told him, hiding his own disappointment. 'I'll be back soon and then they won't be able to stop us.'

Philippe was disappointed not to have Neymar

there alongside him but he was determined to make the most of his big opportunity. On match day, his hard work in training was rewarded – he was in the starting line-up with amazing players like Dani Alves, Thiago Silva, Lucas, Robinho and Alexandre Pato.

It was a very nice surprise indeed. 'Wow, I was sure that I'd be on the bench!' he told his dad.

It wasn't Philippe's best-ever performance but he showed lots of energy and creativity on the left wing. When Menezes took him off at half-time, he was exhausted but satisfied with his start.

'The first match is always the hardest, isn't it?' he reported back to Neymar. 'Next time, I'll make sure that I get more involved.'

Philippe really hoped there would be a next time but he had a long wait ahead of him. Before that, he was called up to the Brazil squad for the Under-20 World Cup in Colombia in the summer of 2011. Neymar was starring for the senior team at the Copa América but Philippe was surrounded by other familiar faces.

'It's time to make up for that awful Under-17

tournament!' Casemiro reminded him immediately. That was a disaster that they would never forget. 'Do you remember how good you were at the 2009 South American Championships? We need *that* Phil!'

Philippe smiled. After his first season in Italy, it was nice to be back with his Brazilian friends. In between the tough practice sessions, they had lots of fun together.

They started the Under-20 World Cup with a 1-1 draw against Egypt. Philippe set up the goal with a corner-kick that landed right on Danilo's head. The team needed more of his creativity in their second game, against Austria. In the first half, Oscar passed to Philippe, who passed back to Oscar, who passed to Henrique, who scored. 1-0!

'Simple!' Philippe said to Oscar as they high-fived. They were forming a great partnership.

In the second half, Philippe scored a penalty and then his cheeky flick helped make it 3-0. It was a magical display.

'That's the Phil I was talking about!' Casemiro joked.

Against Panama, they did it all over again. Philippe passed to Oscar, who passed to Henrique, who scored. Philippe then scored two excellent goals to make it 3-0. He was really enjoying himself.

'You'll score soon, I promise,' he reassured Oscar with a hug.

By the second week, Philippe felt like he was playing with heavy legs but Brazil made it all the way to the final. If they could beat Portugal, they would be crowned World Champions.

'Good luck!' Neymar texted Philippe.

The night before the big match, Casemiro gave his scouting report. 'They don't score very many goals but they haven't conceded a single one yet!'

'Yet,' Philippe repeated. 'They haven't faced *us* yet!'

Brazil felt very confident about winning. Henrique was in great goalscoring form and Philippe and Oscar were the best playmakers in the tournament. Early on, Oscar curled a long free-kick into the penalty area. The ball flew past everyone except one of Portugal's defenders, who deflected it into his own bottom corner. 1-0 – what a start!

'That's *my* goal,' Oscar announced and no-one argued with him.

But Portugal quickly equalised and then took the lead. Philippe was desperate to help his team but he didn't have any energy left.

'If you get the chance, shoot!' he told his replacement, Dudu.

That's exactly what he did. The keeper made a good save but Oscar scored the rebound. 2-2 – what a relief! On the bench, Philippe pumped his fists and cheered.

'Come on, one more goal!'

In extra time, Oscar dribbled down the right wing. As a defender came in for the tackle, he decided to shoot. The ball sailed over the goalkeeper's head and into the back of the net. 3-2!

When the referee blew the final whistle, Philippe raced onto the pitch and jumped on Brazil's hat-trick hero.

'Did you really mean that last goal?' he teased, thinking about Ronaldinho's free-kick. 'Or was it a cross that went wrong?'

'Shut up!' Oscar laughed. 'I meant to score all three of those goals!'

After a brilliant start to the competition, Philippe's form had faded but that didn't matter. It was a team effort and he had a shiny winner's medal around his neck. It was the happiest moment of his football career so far. As they lifted the Under-20 World Cup trophy, silver confetti filled the air. Up on the stage, Philippe, Oscar, Casemiro and the others danced the special night away.

'Do you know who played in this tournament twelve years ago and didn't win it?' Casemiro asked Philippe.

'No, who?'

'Your hero, Ronaldinho!'

## CHAPTER 14

# ESCAPE TO ESPANYOL

'I just want to play regular football!' Philippe said to Aine.

After the joys of winning the Under-20 World Cup with Brazil, his 2011–12 club season wasn't going well at all. The new Inter manager Claudio Ranieri liked Philippe's talent but he preferred to play a 4-4-2 system with wingers. There wasn't much room for a Number 10.

Philippe was on the bench again for the Serie A match against Cagliari, until Wesley Sneijder got injured in the warm-up.

'You'll start on the left instead,' Ranieri told him just before kick-off.

Philippe was really excited; this was his big opportunity to shine. He ran and ran, moving in off the wing to get more of the ball. He was desperate to make a big impact.

Jonathan ran down the right wing, then cut inside and passed across to Philippe on the edge of the penalty area. This was the big opportunity! But Philippe panicked. He hit it first time and the ball trickled wide.

'Stay calm!' Philippe told himself.

A few minutes later, he received the ball again in a similar position. This time, he controlled the ball and dribbled at the defence with his quick, dancing feet. He cut inside and when space opened in front of him, he placed a brilliant shot into the bottom corner.

*Goooooooooooooooooooooooaaaaaaaaaaaaaaaalllllllll llllllllllll!!!!!!!!!!!!!!!!!!*

What a relief! It was Philippe's first Inter goal for months. He had forgotten how good it felt to score in front of the amazing fans. He kissed the club badge on his shirt and his teammate Esteban Cambiasso lifted him up into the air.

'That's the kind of magic everyone wants to see!' Esteban cheered.

As Philippe ran back for the restart, Ranieri gave him the thumbs up. But ten minutes later, he was substituted and for the next match against Siena, he wasn't even on the bench. It was confusing and demoralising.

'If Inter don't rate me, what am I doing here?' he complained to Aine, but she didn't have an answer.

In January, Philippe finally got what he asked for: regular football. He went on loan to Spanish side Espanyol for the rest of the season. He really hoped that the move would be worth it.

Espanyol's manager Mauricio Pochettino met him at the training ground. 'Welcome! I've seen the talent that you have. If you work hard here, we'll give you the experience and confidence to back it up.'

Philippe liked the sound of that. Espanyol were a well-organised team but they needed more attacking, creative flair – namely Philippe's attacking, creative flair.

But at first, with Philippe on board, things didn't go according to plan. Espanyol didn't win a single match in February, and March began with a 5-0 defeat to Real Madrid.

'Don't worry – you're still finding your feet here in Spain,' Pochettino reassured Philippe. He had seen what the little magician could do in training, and knew that soon, he would come to life on the pitch: 'I believe in you. You're a very special player.'

It was so nice to have his manager's faith and support, and Philippe was determined to pay him back. Against Rayo Vallecano, Espanyol were 1-0 up after only four minutes, and Philippe could tell it was going to be a great day. As Sergio Garcia ran down the right wing, Philippe ran to the back post. It was a simple tap-in but he didn't care.

*Goooooooooooooooooooooooaaaaaaaaaaaaaaaaaalllllll lllllllllllllllllllll!!!!!!!!!!!!!!*

Philippe pointed to Sergio to thank him for the pass and then pointed up at the sky to thank God. Finally! He had his first goal for Espanyol.

But Philippe could do better than that. He was used

to scoring beautiful goals. As he dribbled in from the left wing, there were three defenders waiting for him. With a change of pace, Philippe ran past the first defender and then with two magical touches, he dribbled between the other defenders! As the goalkeeper rushed out, Philippe poked the ball through his legs.

*Gooooooooooooooooooooooooaaaaaaaaaaaaalllllllll llllllllllllllllllll!!!!!!!!!!!*

'I feel alive again!' he screamed to his teammates.

Philippe blew kisses to the cheering Espanyol fans. He was really enjoying his time at the club. On the sidelines, Pochettino had a big smile on his face.

And so did Philippe. He was on a roll. A week later, he scored again in another Espanyol victory, this time against Racing Santander. He chested the ball down just outside the box and struck it sweetly into the back of the net. A couple of games later, against Malaga, Philippe took a free-kick. The wall jumped very early and so he kicked it under their feet and into the bottom corner. Another goal!

'That's genius!' his teammate Sergio shouted as they celebrated.

Philippe was working really well with Pochettino. The young Argentinian manager had lots of interesting ideas and he cared about his players. When one of his stars was shining, he was full of praise.

'There is special magic in Philippe's feet,' Pochettino told the media. 'He's Brazilian, after all! Sometimes, his dribbling reminds me of Messi or Ronaldinho. He could be that good one day. And he works very hard for the team too, which is really important.'

In the final game of the season, Philippe wanted to say goodbye in style. He was so grateful to the club and the fans for all of their love and support. They had helped him to find his form again. With fifteen minutes to go, Espanyol were losing 1-0.

Joan Verdú ran down the left wing and played a through-ball for Philippe to chase. The defender was closer to it but Philippe used his amazing speed to get there first. The defender grabbed his shirt but he shrugged him off and kept his cool. As the goalkeeper flew at his feet, Philippe chipped the ball over him and into the net.

*Goooooooooooooooooooooooaaaaaaaaaaaaaaaaaaalll llllllllllllllllllllllll!!!!!!!!!!!!!!*

*Coutinho! Coutinho! Coutinho!*

His name rang out around the Cornellà-Él Prat stadium.

'We're going to miss you!' Joan shouted as Philippe got back to his feet.

'I'm going to miss you too!' he replied.

In six brilliant months at Espanyol, Philippe had learned so much about football and about his own talent too. As long as he worked really hard, he was good enough to reach the top.

'I'm going to miss Spain,' he told Aine, 'but I'm excited about having a few weeks back in Brazil!'

The couple were heading home to get married. During the good times and the bad, in Brazil, Italy and Spain, Aine was always there for him. Philippe didn't know what he would do without her love and support. She meant so much to him. He wanted the whole world to know it, but especially their family and friends.

'It's going to be more like a carnival than a wedding!' Philippe joked on the flight.

Aine pretended to look worried but she trusted her future husband. It was a beautiful day that they would never forget.

Soon, however, it was time to return to Italy. Philippe was ready to fight once more for his place in the Inter first team.

## CHAPTER 15

# LEAVING FOR LIVERPOOL

Philippe ran towards the six-yard box, ready for Diego Milito's cross from the right. When it arrived, he let the ball roll across his body and struck it with his left foot. The goalkeeper was fooled as it flew into the top corner.

*Goooooooooooooooooooooooaaaaaaaaaaaaaaaalllll llllllllllllllllll!!!!!!!!!!!!!!!!!*

'What a start!' Diego shouted as they celebrated. 'That spell in Spain has done you good!'

Wearing the Number 7 shirt, Philippe had come on and scored in Inter Milan's first game of the 2012–13 season.

'Hopefully, I did enough to win a place in the starting line-up!' he told Aine happily.

The starting spot didn't come straight away and when it did arrive, he couldn't make it his own. He was trying too hard to make a big impact. When he dribbled, he lost the ball too often and he kept shooting off target. He didn't get any more goals or assists.

'Stramaccioni took me off at half-time in the Milan derby – that's so embarrassing!' he complained to Esteban. 'What did I do wrong?'

The Inter captain shook his head. 'Nothing, you didn't do anything wrong. We were winning and we needed to make a defensive change.'

But two weeks later against Juventus, Philippe wasn't even on the bench. That was the final straw. He had tried his best to become a star in Milan but he knew now that it was time to move on. He was twenty years old and he would make a name for himself somewhere else.

'I want to be at a club where I will play every week,' Philippe told his agent. 'That's all! I need to get my confidence back.'

When they saw how unhappy he was, Inter tried to persuade him to stay and be patient. 'You're still young and you're still learning,' the coaches said. 'You'll play more games next season.'

But Philippe didn't trust their promises. 'Are any clubs interested in signing me?' he asked his agent.

Liverpool's interest in Philippe had started two years earlier when the club was looking to improve their academy. They wanted to develop great young players for the future.

'We haven't got much money to spend and they have to be Under-21,' the Director of Football Damien Comolli said to Frank McPartland, Head of the Liverpool Academy. 'Any ideas?'

Frank thought for a minute and then remembered. 'I was speaking to Rafa Benitez the other day and he was saying that there's a Brazilian kid at Inter Milan called Philippe Coutinho who's going to be world-class one day. He can play on the left wing or in the Number 10 role. Rafa says that if we act fast, Inter might make a mistake and sell him to us.'

'Great, I'll get our scouts to take a look at him,' Damien replied.

It wasn't easy for the scouts to watch Philippe play because he wasn't getting much game-time in Italy. But, eventually, the Liverpool Director of Football received a series of glowing reports. 'Wow, this kid must be incredible!' he said, showing Frank the responses: 'Dazzling, quick feet', 'Excellent balance when he dribbles', 'Brilliant at spotting a clever pass', 'Great energy and work-rate'. Every single scout said that Liverpool should buy him straight away.

But by then, Philippe had already gone on loan to Espanyol. All the same, Liverpool kept an eye on his progress and now, finally, he was available to buy again. This time they weren't going to miss out. Liverpool's new Director of Football, Ian Ayre, flew to Milan immediately.

'I'm not going home until he's our player!' he told the Italian officials.

But Liverpool weren't the only club in the race to sign Philippe. Pochettino had left Espanyol to become the new manager of Southampton. He was turning them into an exciting team and he was desperate to work with his favourite playmaker again.

'Philippe isn't for sale,' the Inter Milan Director of Football told both clubs at first. But in the end, after days of talking, Inter agreed to let their best young talent leave. They wanted the money to buy new players.

'Wow, they're really going to regret that decision!' Ian thought to himself. It was now just a question of who would win the race to sign him. Liverpool wouldn't give up.

Philippe had a difficult decision to make. On the one hand, he had loved working with Pochettino in Spain, and the manager now had big plans for Southampton which placed Philippe right at the centre of them. But on the other hand, how could Philippe turn down the chance to play for a massive club like Liverpool? They had won the Champions League and that was his dream.

Liverpool too had an exciting young manager, Brendan Rodgers. Rodgers wanted him to play between two amazing players: midfielder Steven Gerrard and striker Luis Suárez. He wouldn't be sitting on the bench any more; he would be their number one playmaker.

'That sounds amazing!' Philippe told his agent. After talking it through with Aine, he had made up his mind; he was going to become Liverpool's new superstar.

Ian was delighted. Now he just had to get the deal done before the transfer window closed.

'We want £10 million,' Inter argued.

'No way! We'll offer you £7 million,' Ian argued back.

Eventually, they settled on £8.5 million. As they shook hands, Ian was sure that Liverpool had just completed one of their best-ever signings.

'What an absolute bargain!' Rodgers said excitedly when he heard the news.

Philippe and Ian flew to England together in one of Liverpool's private jets. At the club's Melwood training ground, they signed the final paperwork.

'I can't wait to get started,' Philippe said, looking around at the brand-new facilities. 'I can already tell that I'm going to love it here!'

## CHAPTER 16

# MOMENTS OF MAGICAL BRILLIANCE

'Welcome!' Steven Gerrard said, shaking his hand.

Philippe smiled. He felt very nervous and shy, especially around superstars like Stevie. It was his first day and they were standing in the entrance to Melwood, Liverpool's training ground. In front of Philippe was the Champions League trophy that Stevie and his teammates had won in Istanbul in 2005.

'Wow, I remember watching that match on TV in Brazil,' he said. 'That was the best final ever!'

Stevie laughed. 'Thanks, but how old were you back then? Five?!'

Philippe shook his head. 'Twelve!'

Stevie rolled his eyes and led the way to the

changing rooms. Philippe wanted to impress his new teammates but he hadn't been playing much football recently. It would take him a few weeks to get back to match fitness.

'*Bem vindo*!' Lucas said, giving him a big hug.

A familiar face! Philippe and Lucas already knew each other because they played together for the Brazilian national team. It would be nice to have a Portuguese speaker around as he and Aine got used to a new country and a new language.

'Don't worry, I'll take you to the only decent Brazilian restaurant in this city,' Lucas joked. 'And we can have barbecues on the two days a year when it doesn't rain!'

Philippe laughed; he was starting to feel more relaxed already. Everyone was very nice to him and he wasn't the only new face at the club. Liverpool had also signed striker Daniel Sturridge from Chelsea. They were way down in seventh place, a massive twenty-four points behind league leaders Manchester United, with fourteen games still to go.

'Rafa says that you can help us qualify for the

Champions League,' Stevie teased. 'No pressure!'

When training began, Philippe could tell that he was slightly slower than usual but his touch and skills weren't rusty at all. The other players looked impressed. In the match at the end, Philippe was put on the same team as Luis. It was only supposed to be a friendly game but Luis was really competitive about everything. He hated losing and he expected a lot from his teammates.

'Play the pass now, NOW! No, too late!' Luis shouted angrily at Lucas.

But he didn't shout at Philippe because there was nothing to shout about. Straight away, they formed a goalscoring partnership. Philippe soon knew when Luis would make a run and where he would run to.

'Great pass, Phil!' Brendan Rodgers clapped on the sidelines. He was feeling good about Liverpool's future.

'Man, it's like watching David Blaine or Dynamo,' Daniel said, impressed. 'You're a proper magician!'

Luis walked off the training field with his arm around Philippe's shoulder. 'This guy is the missing link,' he told Stevie. 'Now that we've found him, we can beat anyone!'

Philippe already felt like a key player for Liverpool – he had the Number 10 shirt after all. Following his struggles at Inter Milan, it was so nice to feel important again.

'I can't wait to play in front of the fans at Anfield!' Philippe told Aine.

Two weeks later, in February 2013, he was a substitute for the home match against West Bromwich. Daniel had made a great start at Liverpool and Philippe wanted to do the same. He couldn't bear to watch from the sidelines any longer. In the second half, he was told to warm up along the touchline.

'This must mean I'm coming on!' he thought to himself. He tried not to get too excited yet, though.

With fifteen minutes to go, Stevie's penalty was saved. Rodgers kicked the air in frustration and then turned to the bench. It was still 0-0 and Liverpool needed a matchwinner.

'Get ready!' the manager called to Philippe.

He was buzzing as he ran on to the field. The fans cheered loudly for their new hero. They had heard great things about Philippe and they needed his magic.

Unfortunately, it turned out to be a debut to forget. West Brom scored two late goals and won the game.

'I hardly had time to do anything!' Philippe complained after the game. He was disappointed with his performance.

Aine disagreed. She was always her husband's biggest fan. 'No, your shot was going in if that defender hadn't thrown himself in the way. Next time, you'll shine!'

Philippe was in the starting line-up for the next match against Swansea City. The Liverpool supporters were excited to see Stevie, Luis, Daniel and Philippe in the same team.

'They're expecting lots of goals and so am I,' Rodgers told the players before kick-off.

At the start of the second half, Luis played a clever through-ball for Philippe to run on to. He dribbled at the Swansea centre-back, who had no idea which way to move. With incredible balance and speed,

Philippe shifted the ball to the right and fired a shot at goal. The keeper dived to the left but the ball flew into the opposite corner.

*Goooooooooooooooooooooaaaaaaaaaaaaaaaaaaalll lllllllllllllllllll!!!!!!!!!!!!!!!!!*

Philippe jumped into the air and roared loudly. Scoring was his favourite feeling in the world and this one was extra-special. His first Liverpool goal in his full debut! Luis was the first teammate to join him in celebrating.

'This is the start of great things,' he cheered.

After sixty minutes, Philippe was exhausted and happy to be substituted. 'English football is so much faster than Italian football,' he told Lucas after the game. 'You don't even get a *second* to relax!'

But he was really enjoying life in the Premier League. With the ball glued to his dancing feet, Philippe could twist and turn past any defender. He wasn't a selfish player, though. Against Wigan, he set up Liverpool's first two goals for Stewart Downing and then Luis. The Uruguayan ran straight towards Philippe.

'Thanks, what a pass!' Luis screamed.

'No problem, it's the least I could do after your pass to me against Swansea,' Philippe replied. It was all about working together as a team.

This time, Philippe lasted seventy minutes before coming off. Slowly, he was getting fitter. 'One day, hopefully I'll be able to play the full ninety minutes!' he joked to Stevie.

'That can wait until next season,' the Liverpool captain replied. 'For now, we're very happy to have your moments of magical brilliance!'

## CHAPTER 17

# RACE FOR THE TITLE PART I

Jordon Ibe dribbled in from the left wing. When his path was blocked, he passed across to Philippe. The Brazilian was more than 30 yards away from goal but he was feeling confident. Each shot was getting closer and closer; the next one was definitely going in. The ball flew like a rocket off Philippe's right boot. It swerved past the QPR defenders and dipped down into the bottom corner.

*Goooooooooooooooooooooaaaaaaaaaaaaaaaalllll llllllllllllllllllll!!!!!!!!!!!!!*

Philippe ran towards the fans in the Kop, pointing and clapping. A goal was the perfect way to end his first season at Liverpool. With Stevie and Luis out injured, the Little Magician had stepped up to become the Anfield hero.

'What a strike!' Lucas cheered, giving his teammate a big hug. 'The supporters love you already.'

In his first thirteen Premier League matches, Philippe had scored three goals and set up seven more. It was a very strong start and he wasn't even back to his best yet.

'Just you wait until I've had a full preseason to get ready,' Philippe told Luis. 'I'll be unstoppable!'

'No, *we'll* be unstoppable!' Luis corrected him.

Liverpool's attack was one of the best in the league: Luis and Daniel scored lots of goals, and Raheem Sterling, Philippe and Stevie all created lots of chances with their speed, skill and passing. They were so exciting to watch, but that wasn't enough to win trophies.

'We need to strengthen our defence,' Stevie argued.

Rodgers agreed with his captain, especially when club legend Jamie Carragher retired. Liverpool signed

Simon Mignolet from Sunderland, Kolo Touré from Manchester City and Mamadou Sakho from Paris Saint Germain.

Luis was impressed by the new signings. 'Kolo has won the Premiership twice and Mamadou is a French international. That's the kind of quality and experience that we need to win the league!'

That was the big aim for the 2013–14 season. Liverpool hadn't won the top English title since 1990 – nearly twenty-five years earlier!

Philippe was determined to help his club to become champions again. He was growing up fast. His long, curly hair was gone; now he had a slick, shorter cut that his social media followers loved. And in training, he showed off a new tattoo on his left arm.

'"O Brasileiro Não Desiste Nunca"', Stevie read in his best Portuguese accent. 'What does that mean, Phil?'

Philippe smiled. 'It means "Brazilians never give up"!'

He played every match and now he could play the

whole ninety minutes every time. He caused lots of problems for opponents with his amazing dribbling skills. One defender, two defenders, three defenders – they still couldn't tackle Philippe. There was only one thing missing from his game: goals.

'Relax!' Luis told him. 'You'll score soon and then you won't stop scoring.'

'That's easy for you to say,' Philippe replied. 'You've got eight goals already!'

Luis smiled proudly. 'That's true, but the main thing is that we're winning games. We're only two points behind Arsenal!'

Philippe nodded. They weren't just winning games; they were winning by playing great passing football. And the next match was against local rivals Everton. For many Liverpool fans, the Merseyside derby was the most important match of the season.

As Stevie went to take an early corner, Philippe stood waiting near the front post. But as the ball came in, he made a clever run round to the back post. He lost his marker and Luis' header fell straight to him. It was a big chance but Philippe stayed calm.

He controlled the ball with his knee and volleyed it past the keeper.

*Goooooooooooooooooooooooaaaaaaaaaaaaaaaaalllll lllllllllllllllllllll!!!!!!!!!!!!!!!*

Philippe's face lit up with the biggest smile. His team was winning and he was finally on the scoresheet. The Liverpool fans were going wild at Goodison Park. It was a moment that he would never forget.

'We can do this!' he shouted to his teammates.

But after two defeats in December 2013, Liverpool slipped down to fifth. They had work to do and Philippe was determined to do better.

'If I do a cool trick but it doesn't lead to a goalscoring chance, what's the point?' he said to Lucas. 'It looks great but that stuff doesn't win matches.'

His teammate was shocked. 'Man, are you sure that you're Brazilian?!'

In the crucial part of the season, Philippe became an assist machine. In the second Merseyside derby, he played a beautiful through-ball for Daniel to score.

Just over a week later, Philippe did something even better against Arsenal. He intercepted a pass in his own half and threaded a perfect long ball between the centre-backs and into Daniel's path.

'That was world-class,' he shouted to Philippe as they celebrated a 4-0 lead. 'I'd like more of those passes please!'

With the Little Magician on fire, Liverpool climbed back up the table. Away at Fulham, they were losing 2-1. Philippe got the ball with his back to goal but he quickly turned and dribbled towards goal. In a flash, he had created something out of nothing. With four defenders chasing him, Philippe curled an amazing left foot shot into the net.

*Goooooooooooooooooooooooooooaaaaaaaaaaaaaaaalllll llllllllllllllllllllll!!!!!!!!!!!!!!!*

The Brazilian pumped his fist and ran back for the restart. Liverpool needed another goal. In injury time, Stevie scored a penalty to make it 3-2.

'Well played, lads!' Rodgers told them afterwards in the dressing room. 'We don't give up – ever!'

A year earlier, Philippe had just arrived in England

after a frustrating time in Italy. Now, he was a Premier League star for a team that was chasing the title.

'I'm so glad that we moved here,' Philippe said to Aine.

By the end of March, Liverpool were only one point behind Chelsea. They had won seven games in a row and if they could beat Tottenham, they would go top of the Premier League.

'Come on!' Stevie shouted before kick-off.

Every Liverpool player was full of confidence, but especially Philippe. He was constantly moving, playing neat passes and then moving into space again. In the second half, he got the ball and dribbled towards goal. He had one defender in front of him, one behind and one on either side. It was time to shoot. The ball skidded across the grass and straight into the bottom corner.

*Goooooooooooooooooooooaaaaaaaaaaaaaaaaaaaaallll llllllllllllllllllllll!!!!!!!!!!*

3-0 – game over! As Philippe blew kisses to the Anfield crowd, Luis jumped up on his back.

'Six more games, six more wins,' he cheered. 'Easy!'

## CHAPTER 18

# RACE FOR THE TITLE PART II

It was Liverpool's biggest match of the 2013–14 season so far when, in April 2014, Manchester City's stars David Silva, Yaya Touré and Sergio Agüero came to Anfield for a huge title showdown.

'We've only lost once at home all season,' Liverpool manager Brendan Rodgers told his players in the dressing room before kick-off. 'Listen to those fans – this is our home!'

Philippe could hear the supporters singing 'You'll Never Walk Alone' through the walls. They were so loud! He felt the goosebumps rising up around his neck once again. There was always a special atmosphere at Anfield but this was going to be extra-special.

Rodgers knew lots of clever ways to motivate his players. At the start of the season, he collected letters from each player's mum. Before each game, he read one out to the team. Philippe was still waiting to hear Esmerelda's words.

Rodgers took out a letter and began reading. 'Son, I'm sorry I can't be there with you in England but I think about you every day. I miss you so much but I know that you are doing amazing things on the football field.'

The players listened carefully and looked around. Whose letter was it? Philippe wasn't yet sure.

'I love you so much, Philippe, and I'm so proud of you.'

He could feel the tears filling his eyes. His mum was many miles away in Brazil but she was also right there with him at Anfield. It was so nice to hear her words of support. Philippe knew that he wouldn't have achieved anything without his family. Sitting there in the dressing room, he felt very emotional but also very inspired. He wouldn't let his mum down.

Liverpool started well, just like they always did. Philippe was at the centre of their fast, passing football. He flicked the ball to Luis who played a great through-ball to Raheem. Raheem fooled the defender and calmly slotted past the keeper. 1-0! As Raheem and Luis hugged on the grass, Philippe was the first to pile on top. Their team spirit had never been stronger.

'Come on!' he roared at the happy fans above.

When Martin Škrtel scored a second, it looked like the game was over. But in the second half, Manchester City fought back to 2-2. That wasn't good enough, though; Liverpool needed to win to stay top of the Premier League. Some of their heads began to drop but Stevie wasn't giving up.

'One more goal!' he shouted. 'Phil, we need another of your moments of magical brilliance!'

Philippe thought back to his mum's letter. Esmerelda was already proud of him but he wanted to make her even prouder. There was still time to be the matchwinner.

With fifteen minutes to go, Vincent Kompany went to clear the ball and sliced it. As it landed in the penalty area, Philippe was the first to react. He knew that he wouldn't have time to control it. There were defenders everywhere. No, it would have to be a first-time shot.

Philippe aimed for the bottom corner and struck the ball beautifully. It flew through the air and then dipped and skipped past the goalkeeper.

*Goooooooooooooooooooooooaaaaaaaaaaaaaalllllllllll llllllllllllllllllllll!!!!!!!!!!!!!!!*

He had scored one of his best goals in the most important match of his career. It was the best feeling ever. Philippe ran towards the fans, pumping his fists and screaming with joy. Near the corner flag, Luis, Stevie and the other players caught up with him. Even when he was at the bottom of the sweaty team hug, Philippe couldn't stop smiling.

'That was goal of the season!' Luis cheered and everyone agreed. Even Philippe's brothers couldn't argue about that.

At the final whistle, Stevie couldn't hold back

the tears. Liverpool were so close to their first ever
Premier League title. It was a match that none of
the fans and players would ever forget. Before they
left the field, Stevie got everyone together for a team
huddle.

'We can't let this slip,' the captain told them. 'Four
more wins!'

'Four more wins!' Philippe and the other players
shouted back.

Against Norwich, Philippe set up Raheem, and
then Raheem set up Luis. 2-0!

'Easy!' Luis joked as they celebrated.

But yet again, Liverpool defended badly in the
second half. They won 3-2 but Rodgers still wasn't
happy.

'If we're sloppy like that against Chelsea next
week, they'll punish us!' he warned.

Chelsea were close behind them in the table.
Philippe knew that it was going to be their biggest
battle yet, even bigger than the Manchester City
match. Could he be the hero again?

As the Liverpool players walked out on to the

Anfield pitch, all they could see was red and white.
And all they could hear was 'You'll Never Walk
Alone'.

'They really are the best fans in the world,'
Philippe thought to himself. They deserved a Premier
League title and he was doing his best to win it for
them. 'Just three more wins.'

Early on, Luis dribbled down the right wing
and looked up for the pass. He spotted Philippe's
clever run down the left wing and crossed to the
back post. Philippe was unmarked but it was a very
difficult chance on his weaker left foot. His technique
would have to be perfect to score with a volley. But
Philippe's technique *was* perfect!

He watched the ball carefully and struck it with
his side foot. It flew towards the goal… but it hit the
side netting. The Liverpool fans groaned and so did
Philippe. So close!

He tried to create more chances but Chelsea's
defence was very strong. Liverpool would have to be
patient. Just before half-time, Stevie dropped deep
to receive the ball. But at the crucial moment, he

slipped. Anfield fell silent as Demba Ba ran through and scored.

'Don't worry – we've still got plenty of time to score!' Luis said, trying to cheer Stevie up.

Philippe created chance after chance for his teammates. But Stevie's long-range shot was saved and then Luis' leg couldn't quite reach Philippe's clever cross. The Liverpool fans groaned again and put their hands on their heads. In the last minute, Chelsea made it 2-0.

As he walked off the pitch, Philippe couldn't believe it. After all their hard work, the Liverpool dream was now in serious danger.

'We were really unlucky today but we have to focus on our last two games,' Rodgers said to the disappointed dressing room. 'If we win them both, we can still win the league!'

Against Crystal Palace, Liverpool were 3-0 up. The victory looked safe but instead of defending, they just kept attacking. Fifteen minutes later, the match ended 3-3. The Liverpool players and fans couldn't believe it. Luis sat down on the grass, crying into his shirt. Philippe was too shocked to cry.

'We threw it away,' he told Aine the next day, once the news had sunk in. He had had a very bad night's sleep. 'What were we thinking?!'

Liverpool won their final match but so had Manchester City. It was so disappointing to finish second.

'I know it hurts right now but you should all be very proud of yourselves,' Brendan Rodgers told his players. 'What a season! We just didn't have quite enough experience to win it in the end. Next season, we'll come back older, better, stronger!'

Philippe nodded. He wouldn't stop until he had that Premier League winner's medal around his neck.

## CHAPTER 19

# BRAZILIAN SUMMER

The people of Brazil had been waiting a long time
for June 2014. Sixty-four years after the disastrous
final of 1950 – played at the Maracanã stadium
near Philippe's childhood home – the World Cup
was finally taking place in Brazil again. This time,
they vowed they were going to lift the famous Jules
Rimet trophy on home soil. It was the only thing that
anyone was talking about.

'I can't believe our brother might be playing!'
Cristiano said to Leandro when the Coutinho family
visited England.

Philippe had grown up watching Brazil in the
World Cup. Romário, Ronaldo, Ronaldinho, Kaká,

Robinho – Philippe was desperate to be the next
national hero. But despite his brilliant season for
Liverpool, he was pretty sure that the Brazilian
manager Luiz Felipe Scolari wouldn't select him for
the World Cup team. There were only twenty-three
spaces in the squad and Oscar, Willian and his good
friend Neymar had all played lots of times for Brazil.

'I made my debut four years ago and I haven't
played since,' he told Lucas. 'Scolari just doesn't
like me!'

'If he doesn't pick you, he's an idiot!' his Liverpool
teammate replied. Lucas himself hadn't played for
Brazil for over a year.

In the end, Philippe was right. When Scolari
announced his squad in May, he wasn't there and
neither was Lucas.

'Oh well, we'll just have to watch it together on
TV!' Lucas joked. He was trying to make Philippe
feel better because he could tell that he was very
disappointed.

Neymar sent Philippe a text. 'Sorry mate, we'll
play together next time – 2018!'

He was grateful for his friend's support. Neymar always inspired him to keep fighting and keep improving. It would be a difficult summer but Philippe would still watch and cheer for his country and his mate. And he would be ready to play in the next World Cup. 'Thanks, good luck!' he messaged Neymar back.

When Philippe watched Brazil lose 7-1 to Germany in the semi-finals, he was quite glad that he hadn't made the squad. It was a humiliating defeat and the fans were furious. They believed that the players had let their country down.

Neymar had missed the crucial match because of an injury. Philippe sent him a text saying get well soon. 'Bring on 2018!' he wrote at the end. They had to think ahead to the future.

'You had a lucky escape!' Lucas said to Philippe in preseason training. 'With Scolari gone, the new manager will want to bring in new players. That's you!'

The new manager was Dunga, who had also coached Brazil at the 2010 World Cup. In August 2014, he announced his squad for the friendlies against Colombia and Ecuador. Philippe was in.

'Congratulations, son!' José Carlos said when he gave him the good news on the phone. His father sounded so happy that he might cry.

On the flight to Brazil, Philippe started to feel nervous. What if he didn't play well? What if he didn't play at all? He didn't usually doubt his own talent but playing for his country meant so much to him. He wanted to shine.

Luckily, when Philippe arrived, there was a friendly face to greet him.

'Welcome back!' Neymar shouted, giving him a big hug.

Philippe felt better straight away. It was like the Under-20 World Cup all over again. In training, the pair showed off all their tricks and played one-twos until they scored. Once training was over, Philippe and Neymar played one-on-one and tried to out-skill each other. They were always laughing and challenging each other.

'It's good to be playing with you again!' Philippe said with a big smile on his face.

Against Colombia, he waited impatiently on the bench. In the second half, it was still 0-0. Brazil needed his magic. With twenty minutes to go, Philippe finally came on for his second international cap. It had been a long wait but it was definitely worth it. Wearing the famous yellow shirt, Philippe ran and ran and ran. He was desperate to do something special. But it was Neymar who scored the winner with an amazing free-kick. Philippe ran to celebrate with his mate. He was so pleased to be part of the Brazil team again.

And this time he was there to stay. A month later, Philippe came on at half-time in a friendly against Japan. They were already winning 1-0, thanks to another Neymar goal.

'I'm going to help you score more!' Philippe told him confidently.

Philippe sprinted infield to win the ball. Then he dribbled forward into space. As the Japanese defenders backed away, Neymar made his run. Philippe knew exactly where his friend would go. They had practised this since they were fourteen years old. The weight of

Philippe's pass was perfect. Neymar took one touch and shot past the keeper. 2-0!

Neymar pointed to Philippe. 'Thanks!' he shouted as they high-fived and hugged.

Later on, Philippe got the ball on the edge of the penalty area. He shifted it on to his right foot and hit a curling shot. The goalkeeper made a good save but Neymar was there to score the rebound. 3-0, and he had his hat-trick!

'Thanks again!' he shouted to Philippe.

Their partnership was lethal and it would only get better. After the disappointment of the 2014 World Cup, Philippe could see happy times ahead – for him, for Neymar, and for the whole of Brazil.

## CHAPTER 20

# LIVERPOOL LIFE WITHOUT LUIS

As Philippe got ready for the 2014–15 Premier League season, he received some really bad news. Luis was leaving Liverpool to join Messi and Neymar at Barcelona.

'No, you can't go!' Philippe complained. 'We're going to challenge for the title again this year and we can't do that without you.'

Luis looked sad but he had already made up his mind. 'I'm sorry but I can't say no to Barca! Besides, you're ready to take over as Liverpool's superstar.'

Then Luis turned to Stevie. 'Make sure you look after Phil, okay? He's the future!'

Philippe was now twenty-two years old. He felt

settled in England and ready to step up and become his team's best player. As one friend left, another friend arrived. Alberto Moreno was an exciting left-back from Spain. He was the same age as Philippe and they got on really well right from the start.

'Hi, I'm Philippe,' he said, offering his hand for the shake.

Alberto smiled. 'Don't worry, I've heard all about you. The guys at Espanyol say that you could be as good as Messi one day!'

Alberto was one of eight new Liverpool signings. The dressing room felt different but Philippe still had Stevie, Raheem, Lucas and Daniel around him.

'We can do this without Luis!' Stevie told his teammates. There wasn't much time left in his career to win the Premier League. It was now or never.

But it took time for the new team to gel. Without their star strike partner, Daniel and Raheem didn't score as many goals. Philippe kept creating chances for them but their shooting confidence was gone. And without Carra, the defence didn't look so strong. By December 2014, Liverpool were all the way down in tenth place.

'Come on, we're so much better than this!' Stevie screamed in the Anfield dressing room before the Arsenal match. 'We can still turn this season around!'

Philippe thought back to what Luis had said to him before he left. It was time to grow up and take more responsibility for the team. They needed more of his moments of magical brilliance. Philippe looked for the gaps between the Arsenal defence and midfield, and waited to pounce.

Just before half-time, Jordan Henderson passed to him on the edge of the penalty area. This was it; in a flash, Philippe came alive. He dropped his shoulder and dribbled cleverly between two defenders to create space for the shot. He struck the ball low and hard towards the bottom corner. It clipped the inside of the post and bounced into the net.

*Gooooooooooooooaaaaaaaaallllllllllllllllllllllllll!!!!!!!!!*

'Come on!' Philippe shouted to the fans, letting out all of his anger and frustration.

Lucas hugged him and tried to calm him down. 'Wow, I've never seen you so passionate – it's scary!'

Philippe was on fire. Against Swansea, he linked up beautifully with Alberto on the left. Drag-backs, flicks, nutmegs – they did them all and there was nothing that Swansea could do to stop them. Alberto scored the first goal and Philippe set up Adam Lallana's second goal to make it 4-1.

Suddenly, Liverpool were flying again. When Philippe scored a swerving, dipping 30-yard screamer against Southampton, his team moved up to sixth place in the table.

'That's more like it!' Stevie said with a smile.

Next up were Philippe's favourite opponents: Manchester City. Could he be the hero again? He was certainly in match-winning form.

'If I get the space to shoot, I'll score,' he said confidently. 'My right foot is a magic wand at the moment!'

After seventy-five minutes, the score was 1-1. Liverpool needed to score again. Raheem passed to Philippe on the left, and he cut inside. He was looking for the goal and he knew exactly where it was. Philippe's shot curled past the goalkeeper's diving arms and into the top corner.

*Goooooooooooaaaaaaaaaaaalllllllllllllllllllll!!!!!!!!!!!!!!!!!!*

It was his best strike yet! Philippe slid along the grass on his knees. Important goals were his favourite goals, especially at home at Anfield. That was a really special feeling. As he smiled up at the cheering fans, his teammates piled on top of him.

*Coutinho! Coutinho! Coutinho!*

Liverpool had the lead; now they just had to defend. Philippe never stopped running. He closed down the Manchester City defenders and made some key tackles. It was all a big team effort. By the final whistle, Philippe was exhausted.

'What a performance!' Jordan told him, giving him a big hug.

Philippe was named man of the match and there was more good news to come. He was on the shortlist for both the PFA Young Player of the Year and PFA Player of the Year awards. Plus, he was in the PFA Team of the Year.

'Me, Eden Hazard and Alexis Sánchez in the same midfield? Amazing!' Philippe said to Stevie when they looked at the line-up. 'I hope Nemanja Matić is ready to do a lot of defending for us!'

Philippe and Stevie dressed up in suits to attend the fancy ceremony in London. Sadly, Stevie was leaving England to play for LA Galaxy in the USA.

'First Luis and now you,' Philippe said with a sad face. 'Who else is going to leave me?'

He would miss his inspirational captain. They had a fun time together at the event. In the end, Philippe didn't win either award but he was still very pleased with his progress. The players and managers of the Premier League had voted for him as one of the six best players of the season. Philippe was very proud of that. And he would never forget the words of Brazil's greatest ever legend.

'Coutinho has a great future,' Pelé told the media when he visited England. Philippe wanted to get the quotation framed on their living room wall.

'That future is now,' he told Aine when he got home. Playing for Liverpool had brought all of his self-confidence back. 'Next season, I'm going to win trophies!'

## CHAPTER 21

# THE BRAZILIAN BOYS

'Welcome to the Brazilian Boys!' Philippe said with a big smile.

Roberto Firmino had just signed for Liverpool from 1899 Hoffenheim in Germany. Philippe had played with Roberto before for the Brazilian national team. He was a brilliant attacker and now they got to play together at club level too. Roberto was allowed straight into the gang.

'Hey, what about me?' Alberto asked grumpily. 'I'm not Brazilian, so why do we have to be called the Brazilian Boys?'

Lucas was the first to reply. 'Well, it's three against one now, so we can call ourselves whatever we want!'

Philippe was very excited about the new season. What he needed was a really good start. Away at Stoke City for the first game, Liverpool found it difficult to create chances. Philippe had been quiet for most of the game and he thought he might be substituted. But instead it was Jordon Ibe who came off for Roberto.

'Let's put some flair into this boring game!' he shouted to Philippe as he ran on.

Roberto was right; it was time for something special. He dropped deeper to get the ball. As it came to him, Steve Sidwell tried to get there first. But Philippe spun beautifully and dribbled towards goal. Was he too far out to shoot? If he missed, his teammates would criticise him for wasting a good chance. But if he scored, he would be the Liverpool hero. He struck it perfectly and it sailed over the goalkeeper and into the net.

*Gooooooooooooooooooooooooooaaaaaaaaaaaaaaalllll llllllllllllllllllllll!!!!!!!!!!!!*

'Phil to the rescue!' Emre Can shouted with joy.

Philippe had never been so determined to win

every game. Against West Ham a few weeks later,
Liverpool were losing 2-0 and he was becoming
more and more frustrated. Just before half-time,
Philippe got a yellow card.

'Come on, that's a warning,' Brendan Rodgers told
him in the dressing room. 'Calm down and play your
natural game. You're not a dirty player! We can still
win this with your help.'

But early in the second half, Philippe slid in for a
tackle. He missed the ball and kicked Dimitri Payet's
leg instead. The referee reached into his pocket and
pulled out a second yellow card.

'Ref, please don't!' he begged but it was too late.

'Noooooooooooooooooooooo!' Philippe screamed at
the sky. What a stupid mistake! He covered his face
with his hands as he walked slowly off the pitch. It
was his first ever red card and he had really let his
team down. Philippe apologised to everyone after
the game.

'We all make mistakes,' Lucas said. 'Just learn
from it and let's get back to winning!'

After his suspension, Philippe came back stronger

than ever. He set up lots of goals with his brilliant dribbling and clever passes. Defenders knew that he loved to cut inside from the left wing but they still couldn't stop him. His footwork and balance were just too good.

In October 2015, Liverpool got a new manager. Jürgen Klopp had taken Borussia Dortmund all the way to the Champions League final and now he wanted to do the same at Anfield. His teams were famous for playing fast, entertaining football. Philippe was sad to see Brendan Rodgers go but he couldn't wait to work with Klopp and win trophies. Liverpool now had two big games coming up – first Chelsea and then Manchester City.

'This is when I shine!' he told Roberto proudly.

Chelsea took an early lead but Philippe didn't panic. After the West Ham disaster, he couldn't let himself get frustrated again. At the end of the first half, Roberto got the ball and passed it to Philippe on the edge of the penalty area. A Chelsea midfielder ran towards him but he skipped straight past him.

'Olé!' the Liverpool fans cheered, rising from their seats.

Philippe was on his weaker left foot but it didn't matter. He steadied himself and curled a beautiful shot into the net.

*Goooooooooooooooooooaaaaaaaaaaaaaaaaalllllllllll llllllllllllll!!!!!!!!!!!!!!!!!!!*

Roberto was the first to run and hug the goalscorer. 'Magic!' was all he said.

'The Brazilian Boys are in business!' Philippe replied with a big smile on his face.

In the second half, the ball fell to him just inside the box. As the defender went to block the shot, Philippe dummied and moved the ball to his right foot. This time he put the ball in the opposite corner of the net.

*Goooooooooooooooooaaaaaaaaaaaaaaaalllllllllllllllll llllllllll!!!!!!!!!!!!!!!!!!!*

Philippe slid on his knees all the way to the corner flag. He had never scored two goals in one game for Liverpool before. What a time to do it! As he jogged back for the restart, he could hear the happy supporters singing his song:

*Olé Olé Olé Olé*
*Coutinho-o-o! Coutinho-o-o!*

With match-winning goals like that, he was quickly becoming a Liverpool legend. It was an amazing feeling.

'Now we just need you scoring too!' Philippe said to Roberto after the game. He still hadn't got a goal for his new club.

Against Manchester City, Philippe dribbled down the wing and passed to Roberto. As Roberto pulled it back to Philippe for the one-two, a defender intercepted. But he kicked the ball straight into his own net. 1-0!

'That's our goal really!' the Brazilian Boys said to each other as they celebrated.

Fifteen minutes later, Roberto won the ball and ran towards goal. Could he see Philippe's brilliant run? Of course he could. When the pass arrived, Philippe coolly side-footed the ball through the goalkeeper's legs. Nutmeg!

*Goooooooooooooooooooooooaaaaaaaaaaaaaaaaalllll lllllllllllllllllll!!!!!!!!!!*

'Right, the next goal is definitely yours!' Philippe told Roberto. They were having so much fun together.

Philippe passed to Emre, who backheeled it back into his path. Liverpool were playing spectacular football. Philippe could have taken a shot himself, but he spotted Roberto to his right. As the goalkeeper came out, he gave Roberto an easy tap-in. 3-0!

'Thanks mate – I scored!' Roberto cheered, flashing his bright white smile. 'I'm so glad the wait is over.'

'No problem,' Philippe replied. 'The Brazilian Boys are really in business now!'

## CHAPTER 22

# TROPHY TIME?

As Philippe went to cross the ball, he felt a sudden pain in his left hamstring. His first thought was 'Not again!' but he tried to run it off. The League Cup semi-final against Stoke City had only just started and Liverpool's Little Magician still had work to do.

'No, I can't come off yet!' he told himself.

Philippe was desperate to help his team to reach the final but his hamstring hurt more every time he tried to get forward. He couldn't carry on; he was only making the injury worse. Philippe gave a signal to the Liverpool physio and lay down on the grass.

'What's wrong?' Alberto asked but Philippe just

shook his head. He was so disappointed. All he wanted was an injury-free season. Was that too much to ask for?

As he slowly hobbled off the pitch, Philippe's teammates patted him on the back. On the touchline, Jürgen gave him a big hug.

'Don't worry, you'll be back soon,' his manager told him. 'We need you!'

The next two months felt like two years to Philippe. He watched from the stands as Liverpool made it through to the League Cup final. At Wembley, they would play against Philippe's favourite opponents, Manchester City. The final was now four weeks away; he had a target to aim for. That was what Philippe thought about every day as he did his boring leg exercises in the gym. With lots of hard work, he could get there.

When the big day arrived, Philippe was back in the starting line-up. After three seasons at Liverpool, this was his best chance of winning a trophy. He was buzzing as he walked out of the tunnel and heard the noise of the crowd.

'Let's do this!' he shouted to Roberto as the game kicked off.

It was a tense match and Manchester City took the lead early in the second half. Liverpool desperately needed one of Philippe's moments of magical brilliance. With time running out, he dribbled towards the penalty area. He passed to Divock Origi and kept going for the one-two. Philippe didn't get the return pass but he stayed in the box. Eventually, Adam Lallana's shot hit the post and bounced out to him for the rebound. Philippe calmly slotted the ball past the goalkeeper.

Gooooooooooooooooaaaaaaaaaaaaaaaaalllllllllllllllllllllllllllllll!!!!!!!!!!!!!!!!!!!!

He was so happy that he took his shirt off and jumped into the crowd with the Liverpool supporters. Philippe didn't care about the yellow card. He had put his team back in the game.

After extra-time, the final went to penalties. Philippe hadn't taken a penalty for ages but he knew that he had to take responsibility. Emre scored but Lucas didn't. The pressure was on.

It felt like a very long walk to the penalty spot. Philippe had a plan in his head but as he ran up, he had second thoughts. He was hoping that the goalkeeper would dive early but he didn't. Philippe's shot was weak and down the middle.

'Oh no!' Philippe wiped his face with his shirt sleeve and sighed. He knew that he would have nightmares about that error for weeks.

A runners-up medal was better than nothing but it wasn't what Philippe really wanted. He moved on to the next challenge – the Europa League. Liverpool were up against their rivals Manchester United in the Round of 16.

'It would be so good to knock them out!' Jordan said with his best evil grin.

In the first leg at Anfield, Daniel scored the first and Roberto scored the second. Philippe jumped up on his Brazilian friend's back to celebrate.

'Now we just need to defend well at Old Trafford,' Klopp told his players.

Manchester United scored first but Philippe knew that an away goal would put Liverpool through.

When he got the ball wide on the left, it didn't look very dangerous. But in a flash, Philippe was in the penalty area, dribbling past the right-back. He just had David De Gea to beat. Philippe faked to shoot towards the far post but instead, he scored at the near post.

Goooooooooooooooooooooooooaaaaaaaaaaaaaaaaallllllll llllllllllllllllll!!!!!!!!!!!!!!

Philippe pointed to the sky and roared. It was yet another special moment to add to his Liverpool collection.

'You're a genius!' Roberto told him.

In the quarter-finals, Liverpool faced Klopp's old club Borussia Dortmund. They were 3-1 down at Anfield but they never gave up. Philippe played a one-two with James Milner and shot into the bottom corner. The comeback was on! In an amazing second half, Liverpool won 4-3.

'What a match!' Philippe shouted as the players celebrated.

Liverpool made it through to their second final of the season. Surely they had to win a trophy this time? Only Spanish team Sevilla were in their way.

The atmosphere was amazing at St. Jakob-Park in Switzerland, especially when Daniel scored from Philippe's pass.

'Come on!' Emre screamed. 'We have to stay focused now.'

But in the second half, Sevilla fought back and won 3-1. Philippe was devastated. The team had worked so hard to get to the final but again, they had lost. It was a hard defeat to accept but soon Philippe was preparing for one last competition of the season: the Copa América.

Since his first international goal against Mexico in 2015, Philippe had been playing regularly for his country. Neymar had chosen to play in the Olympics instead of the Copa América, so Philippe was now a key part of Brazil's attack. After a disappointing 0-0 draw against Ecuador, they really had to beat Haiti. They couldn't let their country down.

Philippe's first goal was his trademark; after a clever turn, he dribbled towards the penalty area and smashed the ball into the bottom corner. Then he scored again with a simple finish.

'I've never scored a professional hat-trick before!'
he told Willian excitedly. Could this be Philippe's
chance? After all, Brazil's manager Dunga had let
his star man play the whole game. Now he had just
thirty seconds left to score. He cut inside and shot
from 30 yards. The ball flew like an arrow towards
the top corner.

Goooooooooooooooooaaaaaaaaaaaaaaaaaaaallllllllllllllll
lllllllllllllll!!!!!!!!!!!!!!!!

It was a very proud moment for Philippe and
all his family. But his celebrations didn't last long
because he still had work to do.

'Now we just need to beat Peru to qualify for the
quarter-finals,' he told his dad afterwards.

But Brazil lost 1-0. Philippe had been knocked out
of yet another tournament.

'I can't believe I didn't win a single trophy this
season!' he complained. He had come so close twice.
It was time for him to take a break and hope for
better luck next year.

## CHAPTER 23

# GOALS, GOALS, GOALS

'Right, I want to win trophies this year,' Philippe told Aine. 'And I want to score goals – lots of goals!'

He had never scored more than eight in a Premier League season, and that had to change. If Philippe was going to play in Liverpool's front three with Roberto and new signing Sadio Mané, he would need to be a proper goalscorer like Chelsea's Eden Hazard or Arsenal's Alexis Sánchez. Philippe certainly had the talent to be that good but he needed to be more consistent.

'Just you wait, I'm better than ever!' he told his teammates confidently.

Liverpool began the 2016–17 season with a difficult trip to Arsenal. They went 1-0 down but there was no need to panic, not when the Little Magician was on the pitch. At the end of the first half, Philippe won a free-kick about thirty yards away from goal. No-one else even thought about taking it. Philippe had practised from this range so many times. He whipped the ball up over the wall and into the top corner.

Goooooooooooooooooooooaaaaaaaaaaaaaaaaaalllllllllll llllllllllllllllllll!!!!!!!!!!!!!!!

'That was the perfect free-kick!' Roberto cheered as the whole team celebrated.

'What did I tell you?' Philippe replied with a huge grin on his face. 'This is my season to shine!'

When Philippe played well, Liverpool played well. He was at the centre of their fast, flowing football. He helped set up the second goal and scored the third himself. With twenty minutes to go, Philippe came off but his teammates held on for the win.

'What a start!' Klopp screamed, giving him a high-five.

By November, Liverpool were top of the league and Philippe had five goals and five assists already. He had raised his game to the next level.

'Let's go and win with Brazil too!' he told Roberto. They always had so much fun playing together.

Brazil's new manager was a big fan of Philippe. 'I remember watching your debut against Iran all those years ago,' Tite told him. 'And I said to myself, "Wow, he's awesome!" And now, here you are playing in my team!'

For the important World Cup qualifier against Argentina, Philippe started in Brazil's front three, alongside Gabriel Jesus and Neymar. It was a big opportunity for him and he was determined to take it. After twenty-five minutes, Philippe got the ball in his favourite area on the left wing. He knew exactly what to do next.

In a flash, Philippe cut inside onto his right foot and left the Argentinian defenders trailing behind him. When he could feel them getting closer, he decided to shoot. Philippe had scored so many brilliant goals for Liverpool but this was even better.

It was an absolute rocket. He couldn't have struck the ball any sweeter.

Goooooooooooooooooooooaaaaaaaaaaaaaaaallllllllllllll lllllllllllllllllll!!!!!!!!!!!!!!!

What a feeling! Philippe had just scored an amazing and crucial goal for his country. It didn't get any better than that, especially with his friend Neymar there to share the moment with him. They ran towards the cheering fans together.

'Yes! Yes! Yes!' Philippe screamed in between each kiss of the Brazil badge on his shirt. He had never been so emotional.

Just before half-time, Neymar made it 2-0. Philippe and Gabriel were the first players to congratulate him and the three of them danced together in front of the fans. Brazil's new attack was destroying Argentina and Philippe was part of it. He felt on top of the world.

'I think that was your best goal ever!' Cristiano told his brother as they celebrated after the game.

Leandro, of course, had a different opinion. 'No way, your goal against Manchester City was way better!'

Unfortunately, when Philippe returned to England, the good times came to an end. He dribbled into the Sunderland penalty area and went to shoot but the defender got his foot in front of the ball.

'Owwwwwwwwwwwwwwww!' Philippe screamed in agony.

He fell to the floor, holding his right ankle. It was more bad luck and just when he was in the best form of his whole career. Philippe was carried off the pitch on a stretcher and the news from the physio wasn't good. He needed six weeks of rest.

'That means I might miss ten matches!' he moaned to Aine as she helped him to get comfortable on the sofa.

'It could have been a lot worse than that,' his wife reminded him. She knew how frustrated Philippe felt whenever he was out injured. 'You'll be back in January, with the best part of the season still to go!'

Philippe worked harder than ever to get back to full fitness. He needed to return to the field as soon as possible to continue his goalscoring form for club and country. But when he did, it wasn't that easy.

Philippe had to start again and rediscover his form. It turned out to be a slow process.

'I don't understand, it's like I'm going backwards!' he complained to Klopp in March. He had only scored one goal since November and Liverpool had fallen down to fifth place.

'Just relax and get the simple things right first,' his manager reassured him. He believed in his star player. 'You'll be winning games for us again in no time!'

But it was only when Everton came to Anfield in April that the real Philippe returned. From that day on, the Little Magician was back to his old tricks. His feet danced and almost every shot seemed to find the net. Against Crystal Palace, Philippe scored another free-kick curler.

Goooooooooooooooooooaaaaaaaaaaaaaaaalllllllllllllllllll lllllllllllll!!!!!!!!!!!!!!!!!!

He ran to celebrate with Alberto on the bench.

'That's your tenth of the season,' his friend told him as they hugged. 'Congrats!'

Philippe smiled but, back at home that evening, he

checked Sánchez and Hazard's stats: 19 goals and 15 goals, respectively.

'I've still got a lot of work to do!' Philippe told himself.

Philippe was Liverpool's Player of the Season, as well as the highest-scoring Brazilian in Premier League history. It had been another successful year for him but he wasn't satisfied. He still had so much more to achieve.

Philippe had left Brazil as a talented teenager with the aim of winning the top trophies in Europe. So far, despite his best efforts, he hadn't won any of them. But Liverpool were getting better and better, and so was Philippe. He was already one of the best players in England and now, thanks to his teammates and coaches, he was close to being one of the best players in the world. Philippe's moments of magic were becoming more and more regular.

The Premier League title, the Champions League, the 2018 World Cup – those were his goals. The Little Magician was now ready to achieve them.

Turn the page for a sneak preview of
another brilliant football story by
Matt and Tom Oldfield. . .

JAMIE CARRAGHER

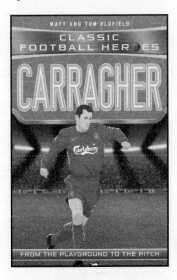

Available now!

**CHAPTER 1**

# GOODBYE, ANFIELD

*19 May 2013*
*He puts his body on the line for the good of the*
*team. His passion stood him out from the rest.*
*He's Bootle's finest and today is his 737th and final*
*appearance for Liverpool. He's the ultimate one-club*
*man. Ladies and gentlemen, please put your hands*
*together for JAMIE CARRAGHER!*

The Anfield crowd was cheering so loudly that he
could barely hear the announcer saying his name.
This was it – the big goodbye. Jamie took a deep
breath and walked out of the tunnel and onto the
pitch for the last time. It was nice to have his two
children at his side: son James wore a matching

Liverpool shirt with '23 CARRAGHER' on the back,
while daughter Mia wore a red and white dress.

The Liverpool and QPR players stood on either side,
forming a guard of honour for him to walk down. As
Jamie walked along, he clapped the Liverpool fans
on each side of the stadium. Playing for Liverpool
wouldn't mean half as much if it wasn't for the club's
amazing supporters.

*We All Dream of a Team of Carraghers,*
*A Team of Carraghers,*
*A Team of Carraghers!*

Jamie would never get tired of hearing 40,000 people
singing his song. The advertising boards around the
pitch all read '23 CARRAGHER, TRUE LEGEND'. The
fans held up red and white cards that between them
formed 'JC 23'.

'Defenders don't often get this much attention!' he
smiled to himself.

Jamie had always known that his final match would
be emotional but he still wasn't prepared for this.

For twenty-five years, he had given everything for Liverpool Football Club. But in ninety minutes' time, it would all be over. Jamie was determined to make the most of his last appearance. With Steven Gerrard out of the squad due to injury, he had the captain's armband.

'I'd have let you wear it today even if I was playing too!' Stevie told his great friend as he presented him with a special trophy. 'I'm sorry not to be playing on your big day but I'll be out there in spirit.'

Jamie and Stevie had won so many battles together with their spirit and determination. They never gave up and the Liverpool fans loved their local heroes for that.

'If you're not careful, it'll be your big day soon too!' Jamie joked, pointing at the sling around Stevie's left arm.

At thirty-five years old, Jamie no longer had the pace to chase after quick strikers but his voice was still as loud and commanding as ever.

'Mark up!' he shouted to his centre-back partner Martin Škrtel.

'Get back!' he shouted to his midfielders Jordan Henderson and Lucas Leiva.

'What a goal!' he shouted to Philippe Coutinho when he gave Liverpool the lead in the first half.

Jamie was relieved. There was only one way that he wanted to end his Liverpool career – with a win and yet another clean sheet.

For sixty-two minutes, Jamie did what he did best. He organised his teammates, keeping them focused and alert. He read the game brilliantly, spotting any danger and making blocks and interceptions. He wasn't letting anyone get past him on his big day.

Then in the sixty-third minute, Jamie did something he hardly ever did. When the ball came to him, he was at least 30 yards away from the QPR goal but he decided to shoot. In that second, Jamie became a striker again, for the first time since he was sixteen years old. He struck it beautifully and the ball sailed towards the top corner… the goalkeeper was beaten… but it hit the post!

As Jamie ran back to defence, he cursed his bad luck. 'So close, what a farewell that would have been!'

With ten minutes to go, Jamie was substituted. The score was still 1-0 but his final victory and clean sheet looked safe.

'Well done, Carra!' Jordan cheered as they shook hands.

The whole of Anfield rose to their feet to clap Jamie as he left the field, including the QPR fans. He didn't want to leave the field but, after a last verse of 'You'll Never Walk Alone', it was time to say goodbye.

As a teenager, Jamie had been one of England's top prospects but no-one could have predicted the level of his success. He had never been the most talented footballer in the world but his amazing attitude and work-rate had taken him all the way to the top. No matter which position his managers asked him to play in – centre-back, right-back, left-back, midfield, or attack – Jamie always gave 110 per cent for the team.

The young Everton fan had become a Liverpool player, and now a Liverpool legend. Jamie had won thirty-eight England caps, two FA Cups, three League

Cups, the UEFA Cup and, of course, the Champions League. There were so many amazing memories that he would never forget – including that incredible night in Istanbul with Stevie, and the FA Cup victory over Arsenal with Michael Owen.

Jamie had so many people to thank – teammates, coaches, friends and, of course, family. He couldn't have achieved his dreams without his mum's support, or his dad's coaching. Then there was his wife Nicola and their children James and Mia. He would really miss playing football but retirement would give him more time to spend with his loved ones.

Jamie's final thanks went to his hometown, the source of his determination, spirit and courage. He would always be so proud of where he came from.

'Not bad for a Bootle Boy!' his dad Philly teased him as Jamie gave one last wave to Anfield.

**PHILIPPE COUTINHO HONOURS**

## Vasco da Gama
🏆 Serie B: 2009

## Inter Milan
🏆 Coppa Italia: 2010–11
🏆 FIFA Club World Cup: 2010

## Individual
🏆 PFA Premier League Team of the Year: 2014–15
🏆 Liverpool FC Players' Player of the Year:
   2014–15, 2015–16, 2016–17
🏆 Samba Gold Award (Best Brazilian Player in
   Europe): 2016

# COUTINHO

**10** **THE FACTS**

**NAME:** Philippe Coutinho Correia

**DATE OF BIRTH:** 12 June 1992

**AGE:** 25

**PLACE OF BIRTH:** Rio de Janeiro

**NATIONALITY:** Brazil

**BEST FRIEND:** Neymar Jr

**CURRENT CLUB:** Liverpool

**POSITION:** CAM

## THE STATS

| | |
|---|---|
| Height (cm): | **171** |
| Club appearances: | **287** |
| Club goals: | **59** |
| Club trophies: | **4** |
| International appearances: | **28** |
| International goals: | **7** |
| International trophies: | **0** |
| Ballon d'Ors: | **0** |

 ★ ★ ★ **HERO RATING: 86** ★ ★ ★

# GREATEST MOMENTS

*Type and search the web links to see the magic for yourself!*

**20 OCTOBER 2010,
INTER MILAN 4-3 TOTTENHAM**

**https://www.youtube.com/watch?v=rfxctqCHOjA&t=236s**

When Philippe first moved to Italy at the age of
18, he found life difficult both on and off the pitch.
However, in this Champions League match, he
showed his amazing potential with two great assists
for Samuel Eto'o and Javier Zanetti. This match will
be remembered for Gareth Bale's hat-trick but Philippe
was another rising star.

## 2 11 MARCH 2012, ESPANYOL 5-1 RAYO VALLECANO

**https://www.youtube.com/watch?v=trvDNDYqxvc**

After a frustrating spell at Inter, Philippe rediscovered his form on loan at Mauricio Pochettino's Espanyol. Philippe scored two goals in this match against Rayo Vallecano but the second was the special one. He tricked his way past three defenders before nutmegging the goalkeeper!

## 3 17 FEBRUARY 2013, LIVERPOOL 5-0 SWANSEA CITY

**https://www.youtube.com/watch?v=DkESVE2mDOU**

Philippe made an incredible start to his Liverpool career. This was his Anfield debut and he scored at the start of the second-half. It isn't one of the best goals that he has ever scored but it was a very special moment. He was off the mark.

## 13 APRIL 2014,
## LIVERPOOL 3-2 MANCHESTER CITY

**https://www.youtube.com/watch?v=cCa96MUnRc0**

Just over twelve months after joining Liverpool, Philippe was challenging for the Premier League title. In a crucial match against Manchester City, the score was 2-2 with fifteen minutes to go. Liverpool needed all three points. Philippe stepped forward to win the match with a perfect shot into the bottom corner.

## 11 NOVEMBER 2016,
## BRAZIL 3-0 ARGENTINA

**https://www.youtube.com/watch?v=w-Mm7cG2gvI&t=434s**

Eventually, Philippe's great form for Liverpool earned him a recall to the Brazilian national team. For the 2018 World Cup qualifier against Argentina, he was picked in an exciting front three with Gabriel Jesus and his best friend Neymar. Philippe took his opportunity brilliantly with a trademark run from the left wing, followed by a stunning long-range strike.

# PLAY LIKE YOUR HEROES

## THE PHILIPPE COUTINHO WONDER GOAL

SEE IT HERE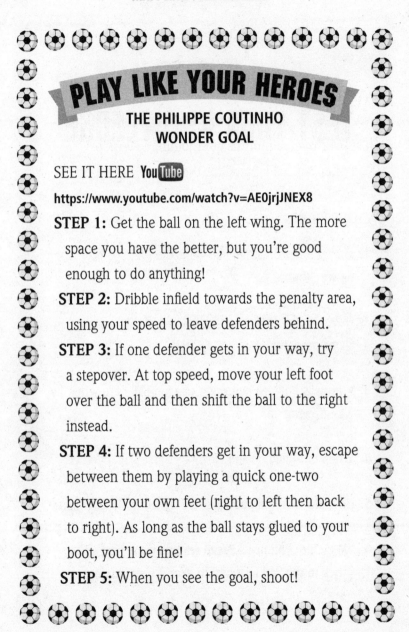

https://www.youtube.com/watch?v=AE0jrjJNEX8

**STEP 1:** Get the ball on the left wing. The more space you have the better, but you're good enough to do anything!

**STEP 2:** Dribble infield towards the penalty area, using your speed to leave defenders behind.

**STEP 3:** If one defender gets in your way, try a stepover. At top speed, move your left foot over the ball and then shift the ball to the right instead.

**STEP 4:** If two defenders get in your way, escape between them by playing a quick one-two between your own feet (right to left then back to right). As long as the ball stays glued to your boot, you'll be fine!

**STEP 5:** When you see the goal, shoot!

# TEST YOUR KNOWLEDGE

## QUESTIONS

**1.** Which other Brazilian ball game did Philippe play when he was young?

**2.** How old was Philippe when he joined the Vasco da Gama academy?

**3.** Who was Philippe's number one football hero when he was growing up?

**4.** When did Philippe and Neymar Jr first play together?

**5.** How old was Philippe when he signed for Inter Milan?

**6.** Which of Philippe's Brazil teammates scored a hat-trick in the 2011 Under-20 World Cup Final?

**7.** How long did Philippe spend in Spain on loan at Espanyol?

**8.** How much did Liverpool pay for Philippe?

**9.** Which Liverpool teammate set up Philippe's first goal for Liverpool?

**10.** Which Brazilian legend said that Philippe had 'a great future'?

**11.** Who are the other members of the Brazilian gang at Liverpool?

**Answers below. . . No cheating!**

1. *Futsal* 2. *83.* 3. *Ronaldinho* 4. *Brazil's Under-14s team* 5. *16, but he couldn't move to Italy until he was 18.* 6. *Oscar* 7. *Six months* 8. *£8.5million — what a bargain!* 9. *Luis Suárez* 10. *Pelé* 11. *Lucas, Alberto Moreno and Roberto Firmino*

# HAVE YOU GOT THEM ALL?

## ULTIMATE FOOTBALL HEROES